Gillian Gilert

Sage 50
Accounts 2011

For users of Sage 50 Accounts, Accounts Plus, Accounts Professional
and the Sage Instant Accounts range

In Easy Steps is an imprint of In Easy Steps Limited
Southfield Road · Southam
Warwickshire CV47 0FB · United Kingdom
www.ineasysteps.com

Notice of Liability
Every effort has been made to ensure that this book contains accurate
and current information. However, In Easy Steps Limited and the
author shall not be liable for any loss or damage suffered by readers
as a result of any information contained herein.

Trademarks
Sage 50® is a registered trademark of The Sage Group plc.
Microsoft® and Windows® are registered trademarks of Microsoft
Corporation. All other trademarks are acknowledged as belonging to
their respective companies.

In Easy Steps Limited supports The Forest Stewardship Council (FSC),
the leading international forest certification organisation. All our titles
that are printed on Greenpeace approved FSC certified paper carry the
FSC logo.

MIX
Paper from
responsible sources
FSC® C020837

Printed and bound in the United Kingdom

ISBN 978-1-84078-417-6

Contents

1 Getting Started 7

Introduction	8
Starting Sage 50	9
Sage 50 Desktop Views	10
Settings	11
Company Preferences	12
Currency & the Euro	15
Customer & Supplier Defaults	16
Finance Rates	18

2 The Customer Ledger 19

Keeping a Financial System	20
The Customers Toolbar	21
Creating Customer Records	22
Price List	24
Batch Customer Invoice	25
Batch Customer Credit Note	26
Debtors Analysis	27
Credit Charges	28
Disputed Invoices	29
Customer Reports & Modem	30
Customer Letters and Labels	31
The Customer Statement	32

3 The Supplier Ledger 33

The Supplier Toolbar	34
Creating Supplier Records	35
Using Search	36
Supplier Activity	37
Supplier Aged Balance	38
Recording Supplier Invoices	39
Supplier Credit Notes	40
Supplier Letters and Labels	41
Supplier Reports	42

4 The Nominal Ledger 43

The Nominal Toolbar	44
The Nominal Ledger	45

Nominal Records 46
Viewing Nominal Transactions 47
The Journal 50
Making a Journal Entry 51
Setting up Prepayments 52
Setting up Accruals 53
The Chart of Accounts 54
Nominal Reports 56

5   The Bank   57

The Bank Toolbar 58
Bank Accounts 59
Bank, Cash & Credit Accounts 60
Recording Bank Payments 61
Supplier Invoice Payments 62
Batch Purchase Payments 63
Bank Receipts 64
Recording Customer Receipts 65
Bank Transfers 66
Recurring Entries 67
Generating Cheques 68
The Bank Statement 69
Bank Account Reconciliation 70
Bank Reports 72

6   Products   73

The Products Toolbar 74
The Product Record 75
Product Defaults 78
Using Search 79
Bill of Materials 80
Viewing Transactions 81
Product Activity 82
Product Adjustments 84
Product Transfers 85
Product Reports 86

7   Invoices   87

The Invoicing Toolbar 88
Invoicing 89
The Product Invoice 90
Printing an Invoice 92
The Service Invoice 93
The Skeleton Invoice 95
Product Credit Note 96

Process Recurring Transactions 97
Updating your Ledgers 98
Printing for Batch Invoicing 99
Producing Reports 100

8 Processing Sales Orders 101

Sales Order Processing Toolbar 102
The Sales Order 103
Allocating Stock 105
Despatching Sales Orders 106
Amending & Printing Sales Orders 107
Sales Orders Reports 108

9 Purchase Orders 109

The PO Processing Toolbar 110
Creating a Purchase Order 111
Placing Orders 'on order' 113
Recording Deliveries 114
Processing Purchases Manually 115
Recording Deliveries Manually 116
Printing Batched Orders 117
Purchase Order Reports 118

10 Financials 119

The Financials Toolbar 120
The Audit Trail 121
The Trial Balance 123
Profit and Loss Report 124
The Balance Sheet 125
Quick Ratio Report 126
The Budget Report 127
The VAT Return 128
e-VAT Submissions 131
Financial Reports 132

11 Fixed Assets 133

The Fixed Assets Toolbar 134
Recording your Fixed Assets 135
Fixed Asset Depreciation 137
Depreciation and Valuation 138

12   The Report Designer   139

The Report Designer   140
Creating a New Report   141
Modifying an Existing Report   144

13   Opening Balances   145

Introduction   146
Standard VAT – O/B   147
VAT Cash Accounting – O/B   148
Clearing Opening Balances   149
Entering Balances Mid-Year   151
Nominal Ledger & Bank A/c   152
Product Opening Balances   154

14   Data Management   155

Backing Up Data   156
Restoring Data   157
Changing Global Values   158
Importing Data   160
File Maintenance   162
Write Off, Refund & Return   165
Posting Contra Entries   168
Run Period End Functions   169
Clearing Audit Trail and Stock   172

15   Task Management   173

Features of the Diary Module   174
The Diary Window   175
Setting Up a Diary Task   176
Setting Up a Recurring Event   177
Completing an Event   178
Chasing Debt   179
Managing Payments   181
Office Integration   182
User Defined Labels   185
Managing Events   186

Index   187

1 Getting Started

This chapter takes you through the stages of preparing Sage 50 for use. It explains initial procedures for setting up Company details and various defaults required by the program.

8 Introduction

9 Starting Sage 50

10 Sage 50 Desktop Views

11 Settings

12 Company Preferences

15 Currency & the Euro

16 Customer & Supplier Defaults

18 Finance Rates

Hot tip

Use the demo data provided to fully familiarise yourself with the program before getting started. To do this simply click File, Open from the main menu and select Open Demo Data.

Beware

Some things, once entered, cannot be easily changed. Therefore, make sure you have all the relevant information to hand before using Sage 50 Accounts for the first time.

Don't forget

You can have a go at setting up a company without affecting your actual accounts data by selecting Open Practice Data from the File, Open menu option.

Introduction

All businesses need to keep accurate accounts. If information is not entered correctly, especially when using a computer program, then the accounts will be wrong – you can't blame the computer!

Working through Sage 50 Accounts 2011 In Easy Steps

This book explains in simple, easy stages how to perform the main tasks required for keeping computerised business accounts. The following chapters show how to:

- Set defaults and Company preferences
- Create customer & supplier records and set up price lists
- Set up opening balances, maintain Bank accounts
- Maintain the Nominal Ledger and run an audit trail
- Generate sales orders and control stock
- Print invoices, credit notes and statements
- Produce history and financial reports

Note: the actual functions available to you will depend on whether you have Sage 50 Accounts, Accounts Plus or Professional. You can even use this book if you work with Sage Instant Accounts.

'Preparing to start' checklist

Before getting started with Sage 50 Accounts 2011, work through the checklist below.

- Check the start date of your company's financial year
- Check with an accountant which VAT scheme is used
- Draw up a list of defaults to use
- Decide on users and passwords
- Backup the data if updating Sage
- Have customer, supplier and bank details to hand
- Product details, recommend a stock take
- A list of all opening balances

Starting Sage 50

Turn on your computer and wait for the Windows Desktop to appear. To start your Sage 50 program do the following:

1 Click on the Windows Start button.

2 Click on All Programs – a selection appears

3 Click on the
Sage Accounts folder

4 Click on
Sage 50 Accounts 2011

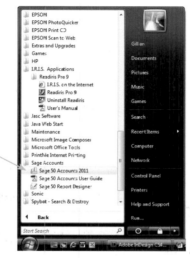

5 The Sage 50 desktop appears

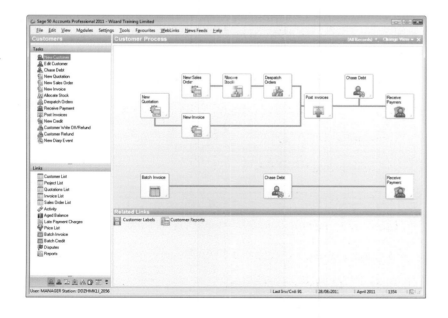

Hot tip

Alternatively, if a shortcut has been set up on the Windows desktop, you can open Sage 50 by double-clicking on the shortcut icon:

Beware

Remember that your reporting will not be accurate until all your opening balances have been entered. Ask your accountant for these, if possible before you start using Sage 50.

Hot tip

You can create multiple delivery addresses so that you can have goods delivered to a number of customer sites whilst specifying a different invoice address.

Sage 50 Desktop Views

In Sage 50, the View selector lets you change the display in the Sage desktop work area. Although the options vary from module to module, typically the views may include a List display, a Process Map and a Dashboard.

A Process Map (Customer) is shown on Page 9, whilst the Nominal Ledger List view is shown below. To switch views, simply do the following:

 Click on Change View

 Select Company Dashboard

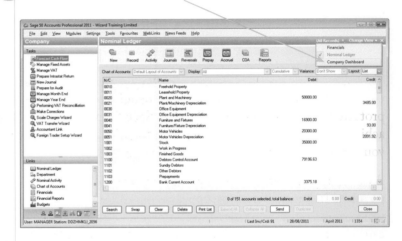

 The Company Dashboard shows important trading information about your business. Click here to print

Settings

Before Sage 50 can be used there are a number of settings and defaults that need to be entered. The rest of this chapter shows how to do this. When required, select the appropriate settings option from the following list:

1 Click on Settings on the Menu bar

2 Click on the option required

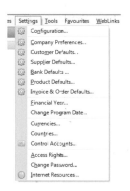

Hot tip

Click Help on the Sage 50 menu bar, then Shortcut Keys, to bring up a list of the available Function Key and Keyboard shortcuts. Click 'X' to close the window.

Using Passwords

The Data Protection Act requires that any system containing confidential information, i.e., financial details etc., should be protected against unauthorised access. Sage 50 uses a password to achieve this. Once you set a password, Sage 50 always prompts you for it at startup.

As with any password, you should avoid writing it down if at all possible. Therefore, try to choose a password that is both easy for you to remember but difficult for someone else to discover. You can decrease the chance of somebody accidentally finding out your password by using a mixture of letters and numbers instead of an actual word.

1 From the Settings menu click on Change Password

2 Type your password here

3 Repeat the password to confirm

4 Click OK to save password

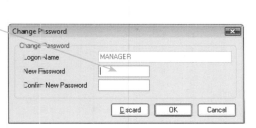

Hot tip

Try to avoid using obvious things like a name, phone number or car registration as a password. These are far too easy to guess.

Beware

If you allocate a password to the logon name MANAGER you must ensure you never lose it otherwise you will have to send your accounts to Sage to have it reset.

Company Preferences

When you run Sage 50 for the first time the Easy Startup Wizard asks for your Company details. Alternatively, after selecting Company Preferences from the settings options, you can enter these details as follows:

Hot tip

Use the Tab key instead of your mouse to move down onto the next line or box.

1 Enter your company name here

2 Enter your full address details

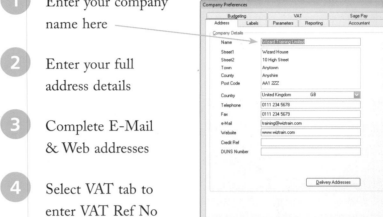

Hot tip

You can enter an alternative address for deliveries by simply clicking on the Delivery Addresses button.

3 Complete E-Mail & Web addresses

4 Select VAT tab to enter VAT Ref No

5 Click OK to finish

Products and Fixed Assets Categories

After selecting Configuration from the Settings options, you can create different categories for dividing products and fixed assets into for analysis:

1 Select tab & click on the first blank entry

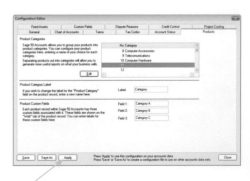

Hot tip

To have Sage 50 print your company details on your stationery, select the Reporting tab and tick the Print Address on Stationery box in the Printing section.

2 Click Edit & enter name

3 Click OK

4 Click Apply button to use

5 Repeat steps 1–4 for Fixed Assets

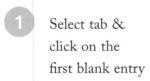

Setting up & checking Tax Codes

Sage 50 already has the standard UK and EC VAT Rates set for you together with the code T1 (standard rate – currently 20.0%) set as the default tax code. Here is a list of the codes automatically set up during installation:

T0   –   zero rated transactions

T1   –   standard rate

T2   –   exempt transactions

T4   –   sales to customers in EC*

T7   –   zero rated purchases from suppliers in EC*

T8   –   standard rated purchases from suppliers in EC*

T9   –   transactions not involving VAT

(* Outside the UK)

There are 100 VAT codes available in Sage 50. To enter or change VAT tax rates, use Configuration from the settings options:

1 Click Tax Codes tab & required code

2 Click Edit

3 Enter percentage rate

4 Tick if VAT rate is for an EC Code

5 Enter Description & click OK

6 Click Apply to use

...cont'd

Financial Year

The start of the financial year is entered during the installation of Sage 50 or before entering any transactions, but it is also possible to change it later:

1 From Settings on the menu bar click on Financial Year

2 To change year select the Change button

3 Click Yes in the next two prompt windows, select year and click OK

Account Status

A handy feature within Sage 50 is that you can assign an account status to each of your accounts. You can add an account status at any time to the ten already set up via the Configuration Editor:

1 Click on the Account Status tab & highlight a blank line

2 Click Edit

3 Enter the Status Name

4 Tick if you want this status to place accounts 'on hold'

5 Click OK, then Apply to use

Currency & the Euro

Sage 50 is already set up with the currencies of 30 major countries, but not the exchange rates. These details can be edited or other countries set up as required:

1 Click on Settings, Currencies and highlight the currency you want to edit or select the first blank record to enter a new currency

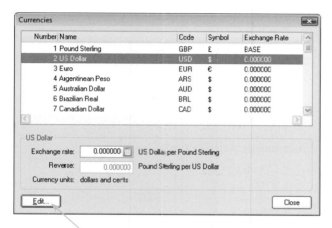

2 Click Edit to bring up the Edit Currency box

3 Enter the name of the Currency

4 Complete the Currency Code & the Currency symbol

5 Enter the Currency exchange rate

6 Enter the Major & Minor currency units

7 Click OK, then Close the Currencies box

Hot tip

Simply press F5 to access the Currency Calculator in any numeric field that displays the calculator button icon.

Hot tip

The calculator can be used to either view an amount converted from Sterling to a Euro/Foreign Currency or to convert a Euro/Foreign Currency amount to Sterling.

Beware

Exchange rates change frequently, so make sure you have the latest rates entered before recording a foreign currency transaction. Up to date rates are available from a number of sources, including the Internet (e.g. www.xe.com).

15

Customer & Supplier Defaults

When creating a new customer or supplier, details about credit limit, terms, discount etc. are needed. Customer and Supplier records are discussed in Chapters 2 & 3 respectively but before this, defaults need to be set up.

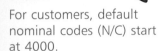

Hot tip

For customers, default nominal codes (N/C) start at 4000.

Don't forget

A customer can be a member of a price list. However, as a customer can only belong to one price list, if you want to change the list that the selected customer belongs to simply choose a different price list from the drop-down list. Note that on each price list, additional discounts can still be applied.

Hot tip

Default nominal codes for suppliers start at 5000.

1 Select Customer Defaults from the Settings options

2 Enter defaults for your customer records on the first Tab

3 Click on the relevant Tabs to enter Statements, Ageing Balance and appropriate Discount defaults

4 Click OK to save the Customer Defaults entered

5 Now select Supplier Defaults from the Settings options

6 Enter relevant Supplier Defaults

7 Use Ageing Tab to enter Aged Balances Period, specifying calendar months or days

8 Click OK to save Supplier Defaults

Product Defaults

Defaults also need to be set up for Products:

1 Select Product Defaults from the Settings options

2 Enter the Nominal Account code here

3 Allocate the correct Tax Code for the Product

4 Complete the rest of the defaults as necessary

5 Enter the Decimal Point placing for the product

6 Click OK to save this information

Control Accounts

Sage 50 uses Control Accounts to make automatic double-entry postings to the ledger.

1 To view or edit these Nominal Codes select Control Accounts from the Settings options

2 To change a Control account click on the nominal code and type the new code or use the Finder button

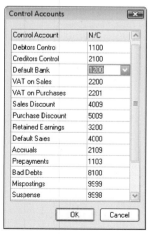

3 Click OK to save and close or Cancel to abandon changes

Finance Rates

Finance rates need to be set up before any credit charges can be applied to your customers.

Hot tip

When a Finance Charge Rate is applied to a transaction, the first rate charged will be applied monthly until the invoice is paid.

Don't forget

You must first have set up your finance rates and the date from which they are to be applied before you can use the Charges option on the Customer toolbar.

Hot tip

Use the Delete button on the Finance Charge Rates window to remove any unwanted charges.

1. Select Configuration from the Settings menu and click on the Terms tab to bring up the Finance Charge Rates box

2. Click on Add to enter a new finance rate charge

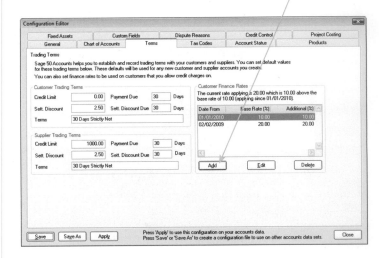

3. Enter the date the charge is to be applied from

4. Enter the Base Rate as a percentage

5. Enter an additional charge if applicable

6. Click OK to save new finance rate or Cancel to return to the Finance Charge Rates box

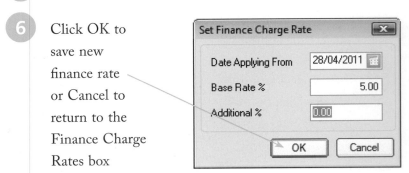

7. Click Close to finish

2 The Customer Ledger

Learn how to use the Customer (Sales) Ledger to maintain customer records and create new ones as well as enter credit notes and invoices. See how to view transaction activity, set up a customer price list, produce an overdue payments letter, apply credit charges and mark an invoice as disputed.

20	Keeping a Financial System
21	The Customers Toolbar
22	Creating Customer Records
24	Price List
25	Batch Customer Invoice
26	Batch Customer Credit Note
27	Debtors Analysis
28	Credit Charges
29	Disputed Invoices
30	Customer Reports & Modem
31	Customer Letters and Labels
32	The Customer Statement

Keeping a Financial System

It is essential for all businesses to have a system to record and monitor their business and financial transactions. This information needs to be accurately recorded and kept up to date if it is to present a true financial position.

Such a system will involve the recording of transactions using the traditional method of bookkeeping or advanced accounting procedures, so that financial reports (i.e. profit & loss statements and balance sheet, etc.) can be produced.

These reports provide the Management with information on sales, purchases, turnover, expenses, debtors and creditors, assets and liabilities, and more importantly, if the business has made a profit.

HM Revenue and Customs will also need accurate accounts, which must conform to general bookkeeping and accounting procedures. This is vital for Tax & VAT Returns. Visit the website at www.hmrc.gov.uk for up to date information on online filing and payments.

This information is also of importance to your Bank Manager, especially if there is a need to borrow money to ease cash flow problems or help set up a new business venture. Likewise, potential investors in your business may first want to see the true financial position of your accounts before making a decision.

Computerised systems have now removed the majority of time consuming and repetitive tasks of manual accounting. Businesses can check their financial status on a daily basis, or over a designated period of time. This valuable information will aid important decision making and business planning and is crucial for forecasting whether a business will succeed or fail.

Sage 50 makes keeping computerised accounts easy. Many of the report templates needed are provided with the package, so producing accurate business reports is a simple matter, provided, of course, that all information has been entered correctly. The following chapters guide you through the processes involved in keeping accurate and up to date computerised financial accounts for your business.

Hot tip

Regularly monitor your Customer credit using the Chase Debt option in the Customer Tasks list. Here you can quickly see who owes you money and easily produce a handy printout of any overdue or outstanding debtors useful for chasing payment.

The Customers Toolbar

The Customers toolbar provides features for creating customer records and viewing transaction activity, producing invoices and credit notes, marking invoices as disputed and applying credit charges. Customer Statements are produced here, plus letters, a range of reports and generating price lists.

New   Creates a new Customer Account

Record   Opens a Customer Record

Price List   To set up a Customer Price List

Activity   Opens Customer Activity

Aged   Opens Customer Aged Balances

Invoice   Opens the Batch Customer Invoices window

Credit   Opens the Batch Customer Credits window

Dispute   Opens the Disputed Items window

Charges   Opens the Credit Charges window

Labels   To print Customer Labels

Letters   To print Standard Letters to Customers

Statement   To print Customer Statements

Reports   To run Customer Reports

Creating Customer Records

In this window, a customer record can be added, edited or deleted. You can record agreed credit terms and even log any contact you have with a customer, such as telephone calls and who you spoke to. You can also record if invoices are sent electronically.

Hot tip

Use the New wizard for easy to follow step by step instructions for entering a basic new customer record.

1 Select Customers from the Sage 50 navigation bar

2 Click on Record to bring up the Customer Record window

3 Use Details tab to store basic customer information

4 Use the O/B button if an opening Balance is required

Don't forget

You cannot enter an Opening Balance until you have saved the new customer details record.

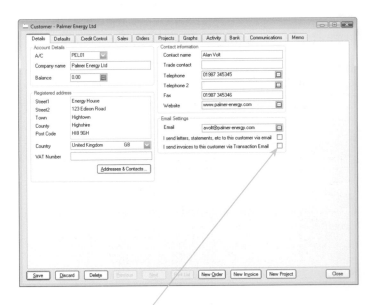

5 Tick here if invoices are sent electronically

6 Use the Credit Control tab to enter any credit terms you have agreed for this customer

Beware

The method of entering opening balances is different for Standard VAT and VAT Cash Accounting. Use F1 help key to check.

7 Click Save to store the Customer Record

8 Enter a new record or click Close to finish

Viewing transactions

Once customer activity has taken place, Sage 50 offers you a
variety of options for checking customer transaction details:

Don't forget

Note that the following
codes indicate the
transaction type:

SI = Sales Invoice
SR = Sales Receipt
SC = Sales Credit Note
SD = Sales Discount
SA = Sales Receipt on
     Account

- View customer invoices, receipts, credit notes and balances
  on a monthly basis, as a graph or table

- Use the Activity option to see a breakdown of each
  customer's transactions

- View or print the Customer's aged balances

1 Click on the Activity tab in the Customer Record window

2 Select a transaction, all items appear in the lower pane

3 Use the scroll bar to move through all the transactions

4 Click on Show to select another range of transactions,
enter dates if choosing Custom Range then click OK

Hot tip

Use the Orders tab to
quickly view a history
of the sales orders a
customer has placed
with you. Simply double
click on an order in the
list to bring up the sales
order record.

5 Select Close to return to Customer window

Price List

In Sage 50, different price lists can be set up and customers allocated to the price list of your choice. For each Price List products can be added and different prices set up accordingly. For example, you can create custom lists for Trade, Retail, Summer or Winter Sales and Special Offers.

To create a new Price List do the following:

Hot tip

Where a selected customer is already on another price list, Sage 50 asks if you want to transfer this customer to the new list. Click Yes to transfer the customer to the new list or Yes to All to transfer all customers already on another list to the new list.

1 From the Customers toolbar click on the Price List button to bring up the Price Lists box

2 Click New to open the New Price List window

3 Enter Reference and Name

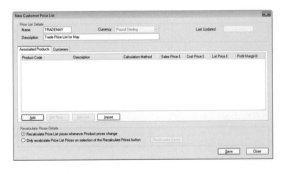

4 Click Save

Hot tip

To add more than one customer at a time to your list, simply hold down the Control key and click on your selection during Step 6.

5 Select Customers tab & click Add to bring up a list

6 Select Customer

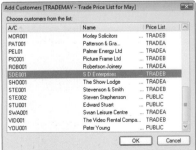

7 Click OK

8 Click Save, then Close and Close again

Batch Customer Invoice

Invoices are important business transaction documents and record detailed information about the goods or services supplied to the customer. Briefly, these details include the invoice number, name and address of the customer, date of sale, details of goods and or services supplied, details of discount, total amount of money due and terms of trade.

There are different types of invoices and Chapter 7 shows you how to create a product or a service invoice, as well as automatically creating an invoice from a sales order. However, any invoices produced manually (Batch Invoices) and sent to customers also need recording. No printout is produced.

To record a batch customer invoice do the following:

1. Choose Invoice from the Customers toolbar

2. Enter the customer Account Code or use the finder button to display a list of codes

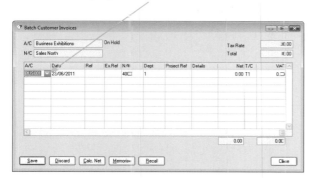

3. Change invoice date if different from current system date

4. Enter the Invoice Number and a Ref. Number, as required

5. Change Nominal Code or Department if different

6. Enter Net value of invoice

7. Click Save to update the nominal ledger and customer details (details posted), then Close

25

Hot tip

Where you only know the gross value of an invoice, enter it in the Net box and use the Calc. Net button (or press the F9 shortcut key) to let Sage 50 work out the correct Net value and VAT due.

Hot tip

For a list of useful data entry Shortcut Keys see the inside front cover at the start of this book.

Beware

Always check that the correct Tax Code is used. See page 13.

Batch Customer Credit Note

A credit note is used, for example, where an error is made and a customer has been overcharged on an invoice. Sometimes, damaged goods are returned and so a credit note is issued showing the amount due to the customer.

Like batch invoicing, credit notes processed manually need to be entered. To record batch credit notes:

Hot tip

To check the credit note has been posted, make a note of the balance for the appropriate customer in the Customers window before entering the credit note, then check that the balance has reduced by the correct amount after performing Step 6.

1. Click Credit from the Customers toolbar to bring up the Batch Customer Credits window

2. Enter the customer Account Code

3. The screen displays the defaults for the nominal account code posting, VAT rate to be applied & department

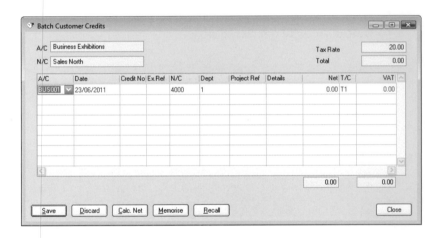

Don't forget

When looking at Customer activity, the transaction type (Tp) code SC indicates a Sales Credit Note.

4. Enter credit details for each customer in the same way as for batch invoice

5. Check all values are correct & click Save to post the details or Discard to start again

6. Click Close to return to the Customers window

Debtors Analysis

To identify debtors and monitor cashflow, customers' outstanding balances and transactions need to be regularly checked. These transactions are grouped by the age of the debt, either on calendar months or based on a period of days, e.g. 30, 60 and 90 days etc. Debt chasing letters can be issued if required. A business may use this information to calculate interest charges for late payment.

1 From the Customers window select the required customer

2 Click Aged to bring up the Aged Balances Date Defaults box

3 Enter the date to be used for calculating the aged balances

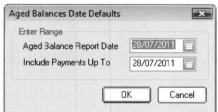

4 Enter the date to include payments up to

5 Click OK to bring up the Aged Balances window

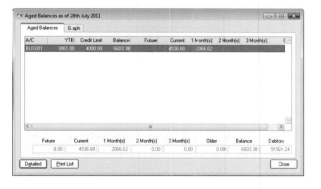

6 To see a graph format click the Graph tab

7 For a transaction breakdown click on Detailed

8 Click Close to return

Hot tip

From the Settings menu select Customer Defaults, then the Ageing tab to change the age of the debt from calendar months to period of days, or vice versa.

Beware

When you select the required customers in the Customers window, always check that the dates in the Aged Balance Report Date and the Include Payments Up To boxes cover those selected customers.

Credit Charges

A payment which is 30 days overdue is regarded, by default, as late. If you need to change payment terms, do the following:

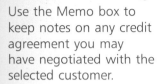

Hot tip

Use the Memo box to keep notes on any credit agreement you may have negotiated with the selected customer.

1 From the navigation bar choose the Customers button

2 Highlight the appropriate customer or customers, then click the Record button

3 Click on the Credit Control tab to bring up the Credit Control details box

Hot tip

To apply charges to customers whose payments are overdue simply click Charges from the Customers window to run the Credit Charges Wizard.

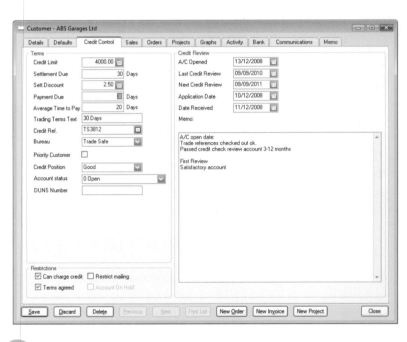

4 Enter new details in Payment Due

5 Apply account restrictions if desired, such as placing account on hold or allowing credit to be charged

6 Change any of the other terms as required, then click Save

7 Click Close to return to the Customers window, then Close again

Beware

Before you can use the Credit Charges Wizard, finance rates must have first been set up.

Disputed Invoices

There may be times when an invoice is questioned by the customer, so until an agreement is made the invoice can be marked as disputed. This option also applies to any invoices not fully paid. Once the problem is resolved, you can remove the disputed flag (indicator). To mark an invoice as disputed:

1 Click on the Dispute button in the Customers window to bring up the Disputed Items window

2 Enter the Customer Account Code and press the Tab key

3 Click on the transaction you want to mark as disputed

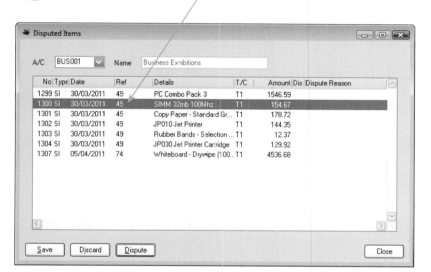

4 Click Dispute

5 Select Reason & Click OK

6 Note that transaction is now marked as 'd'

7 Click Save to record the transaction

8 Click Close to return to the Customers window, then Close again

Don't forget

Don't forget to first set up Dispute Reasons using the Configuration Editor. This will then give you more accurate reporting when you need to check why an item has been marked as disputed in the future.

Hot tip

To remove the Dispute status of an invoice simply highlight it and click on the Dispute button again.

29

Don't forget

Remember that if you are using Standard VAT, invoices marked as disputed are still included in the VAT Return.

Customer Reports & Modem

Sage 50 provides you with a wide range of ready-designed customer reports to suit the majority of needs. To print or view a customer report, do the following:

1 Click on the Reports button in the Customers window

2 Click here on the appropriate folder & select the report you require from the list

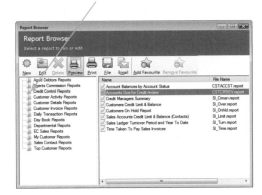

3 Click the Preview or Print button to generate the report

4 After printing Close each window

Modem

For some features, you need to have a modem fitted in your PC. By default, the F11 key is set up by Sage 50 to open the Control Panel so that you can check if your computer has a modem installed, as follows:

1 Press the F11 key to bring up the Windows Control Panel

2 Double-click on the Phone and Modem icon

3 Click the Modems tab to see if a modem is fitted

Customer Letters and Labels

Occasionally, you may have a need to send standard information to a customer, such as change of address, or to chase up an overdue payment. All of the necessary information needed for these letters is taken from your records.

A number of the more common standard letters are provided with Sage 50, but alternatively there is the option to create new ones. The new letters can be stored for future use.

1 From the Customers window, select the customer or customers you want to send a letter to

2 Click the Letters button on the Customers toolbar to bring up the Customer Letters list

3 Click on the letter required

4 Click Preview to view the letter

5 Select Criteria and whether to update history

6 If correct, click Print, then OK

7 Click here to Close

Don't forget

Remember to select a customer from the list before clicking the Letters button.

Hot tip

To send the same letter (e.g. change of address) to all your customers, first deselect all customers using the Clear button in the Customers window then carry out Steps 2–7.

The Customer Statement

To keep customers up to date about their financial position, customer statements should be sent out on a regular basis, normally once a month. The statement shows details of all recorded customer transactions, together with a balance figure.

Don't forget

You can also use the Customer Statement window to delete statements no longer required, or to modify and design your own.

1 From the Customers window first select the Customers you want statements for, then click on the Statements button to bring up the Customer Statements window

2 Choose the statement layout you require

3 Click the Preview button

4 Wait for report to generate and the Criteria box to appear

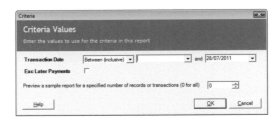

Hot tip

To preview a sample report, simply enter a small number of records in the box provided.

5 Enter Transaction Date From & To

6 Choose whether to Exclude Later Payments

7 Click OK to preview the statement

8 Use the Zoom button on the preview to zoom in or out if you need to check any statement detail

9 Click Print to print the statement, then Close all windows

3 The Supplier Ledger

See how to create and maintain supplier records within the Supplier (Purchase) Ledger. You will learn how to view details of invoices received and payments made to suppliers using graphs and reports.

34 The Supplier Toolbar

35 Creating Supplier Records

36 Using Search

37 Supplier Activity

38 Supplier Aged Balance

39 Recording Supplier Invoices

40 Supplier Credit Notes

41 Supplier Letters and Labels

42 Supplier Reports

The Supplier Toolbar

The Supplier toolbar has many similar buttons to the Customer toolbar, and again provides you with facilities for setting up records, checking supplier activity, recording invoices, credit notes and reporting.

 Creates a new Supplier Record

New

 Opens a Supplier Record

Record

 To set up a Supplier Price List

Price List

 View Supplier Activity

Activity

 View Supplier Aged Balances

Aged

 Record Supplier Invoices

Invoice

 Record Supplier Credit Notes

Credit

 Opens the Disputed Items window

Dispute

 To Print Supplier Labels

Labels

 To Print Standard Letters to Suppliers

Letters

 To Run Supplier Reports

Reports

Creating Supplier Records

Within this window you can view, edit or delete a supplier record. A new supplier record can also be added if you have all of the details to hand. To add a new supplier first select Suppliers from the Modules option or navigation bar, then do the following:

1 Select Suppliers from the Sage 50 navigation bar

2 Click on Record to bring up the Supplier Record window

3 Use Details tab to store basic supplier information

4 Use the O/B button if an opening Balance is required

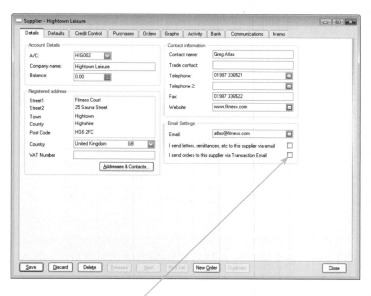

5 Tick here if orders are sent electronically

6 Enter credit terms using the Credit Control tab & the Bank tab to record bank details for payment transfers

7 Click Save to store the Supplier Record

8 Enter a new record or click Close to finish

35

Hot tip

Until you are familiar with Sage 50, use the New wizard for simple step-by-step instructions for entering a new supplier record.

Don't forget

Always start with the Account Code when entering a new record.

Using Search

The Search function available within the suppliers window can help save you valuable time when searching for specific information regarding supplier transactions. The following example shows you how to produce a list of suppliers you owe money to:

1 Click the Search button in the bottom left hand corner of the Suppliers window to bring up the Search window

2 Click Where in the first column

3 Select Balance in this field

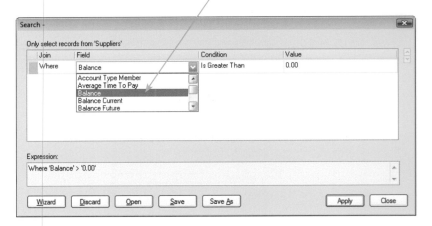

4 Select Is Greater Than in the Condition column

5 Enter zero in the Value field

6 Click Apply & Close to return to the Suppliers window

7 Note that only records matching the search are displayed. The title bar indicates the Search is applied

8 To cancel the search and show all records, click this icon

Suppliers   (10 of 16 Records matched) ○, Change View ▾ ✕

Supplier Activity

This feature enables you to view each supplier's transactions in detail. If less complete information is required, you can define a transaction or date range to limit the view:

1 From the Suppliers window select the supplier you want to look at, then click on Activity

2 Select a transaction, all items appear in the lower pane

3 Use the scroll bar to move through all the transactions

4 Click on Show to select another range of transactions

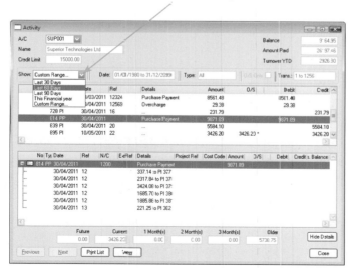

5 Click Close to return to the Suppliers window

Hot tip

To view this screen from the Supplier Record window, enter the A/C for the supplier required (if none selected) then click on the Activity tab.

Hot tip

Double-click on any Purchase Invoice (PI) transaction to bring up the relevant Product Purchase Order.

Don't forget

Note that the following codes indicate the transaction type:

PI = Purchase Invoice
PP = Purchase Payment
PC = Purchase Credit Note
PD = Discount on a Purchase Payment
PA = Purchase Payment on Account

Supplier Aged Balance

Aged balance is the term given to the time lapse of outstanding debt, whether owed to you or by you. Sage 50 lets you view the amount of money you owe your Suppliers, grouped on the age of the debt. It is common practice for businesses to give 30 days credit, but other terms are sometimes negotiated. Sage 50 default aged periods are 30, 60 and 90 days.

1 From the Suppliers window, click on the supplier you require (or ensure none selected to view all) and select the Aged button from the toolbar

2 Enter dates and click OK to display the Aged Balances Report

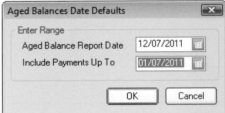

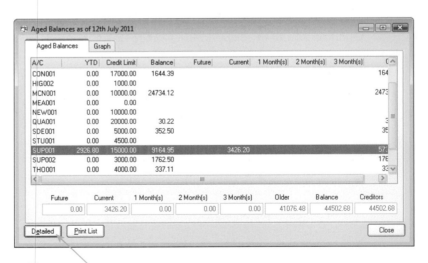

3 To see the transactions which make up the aged balance click Detailed

4 Close each window when finished

Recording Supplier Invoices

Invoices received from your suppliers can be entered a few at a time using the Batch Supplier Invoices window. You have full flexibility using this option, such as posting each invoice item to a different nominal account if need be, or allocating to a different VAT code, such as from default VAT to zero VAT. To enter invoices, do the following:

1 From the Suppliers window click Invoice to bring up the Batch Supplier Invoices window

2 Type the supplier's account code or use the Finder button

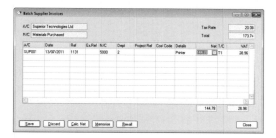

3 Enter the Date and other invoice details, amending the Nominal (N/C) and Tax (T/C) codes if necessary

4 When all details are correct and all invoices have been entered, click Save to post the details then click Close to return to the Suppliers window

5 Note that the Supplier's record now displays the new balance, then click Close again

39

Beware

Always check that the correct tax code has been selected for the VAT to avoid errors later. Sage 50 enters T1 (standard rate) for you by default. You may need to change this to T0 for transactions which are zero rated or to T9 for any not involving VAT.

Don't forget

Remember that with batch invoices, no printouts are generated of the transaction entered. Use activity reports if you require a paper copy.

Don't forget

'Posting' means updating the Nominal ledger and relevant supplier's details. If you do not wish to save this batch, choose the Discard button to clear the data and start again.

Supplier Credit Notes

Occasionally, goods ordered from suppliers may arrive damaged or incomplete. The supplier issues you a credit note reducing the amount owed. Credit notes are recorded using the Credit option from the Suppliers window.

If a credit note contains a number of items, for your benefit it is advisable to enter each transaction individually, but giving them the same account code, date and reference. Sage 50 groups these together and lists them as a single credit note. You can then view the note in more detail using Activity from the Suppliers window.

40

1 From the Suppliers window click Credit

2 Enter the supplier Account Code. Use the Finder button if you don't have the code

3 Enter the credit note Date and remaining details

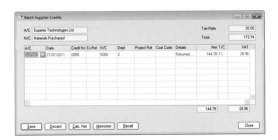

4 Click Save to update the nominal ledger & record the credit details, then Close to return to the Suppliers window

5 Note that the Balance has changed, then click Close

Supplier Letters and Labels

As with Customers, Sage 50 includes the facility to produce preformatted letters and labels for your suppliers. You can create whatever standard letters or label layouts you wish. All necessary address information etc. is taken from the stored supplier details.

For example, to produce the standard letter informing suppliers of your change of address, do the following:

1 From the Suppliers window first select a supplier, then click Letters to bring up the Supplier Letters window

2 Click on the letter required

3 Click Preview and wait for the report to generate

4 Check the letters and click Print, then OK

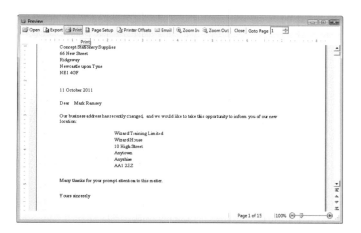

5 When finished, Close all windows

Labels

To produce address labels for your suppliers, click the Labels button from the Suppliers window then carry out Steps 2–5 as above.

Hot tip

The Credit Control tab window has an option to Restrict mailing. Use this to control who you send mailshots to.

Beware

Always remember to check that the correct paper, labels and printer type have been selected before printing to avoid wasting time and paper.

Supplier Reports

You can generate a wide range of detailed reports on your suppliers. These reports are produced from the information you entered about suppliers and their transactions. Sage 50 already has a considerable number of reports set up, but if any further reports are required you can create them using the Report Designer (see Chapter 12). To run or view a supplier report:

Don't forget

A Criteria box will appear when you click Preview or Print on most reports for you to enter ranges, such as Supplier Reference, Transaction Date etc.

1 Click on the Reports button in the Suppliers window

2 Click here on the required folder and select a report

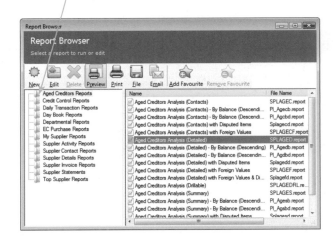

3 Click on the Preview button to begin producing the report

4 If a Criteria box appears, enter the From and To details

5 Tick the Transactions or Payments options as required, then click OK

Don't forget

From the Supplier Reports window you can also edit or delete an existing report or create a new one.

6 After printing, Close all windows

4 The Nominal Ledger

This chapter explains the important role played by the Nominal Ledger and how its contents detail the flow of money in and out of the business. You will be shown how to analyse these account transactions using graphs and activity reports.

44 The Nominal Toolbar

45 The Nominal Ledger

46 Nominal Records

47 Viewing Nominal Transactions

50 The Journal

51 Making a Journal Entry

52 Setting up Prepayments

53 Setting up Accruals

54 The Chart of Accounts

56 Nominal Reports

The Nominal Toolbar

The Nominal toolbar buttons provide you with facilities for setting up records, viewing account activity, making journal entries, setting up prepayments and accruals, working on the chart of accounts and reporting.

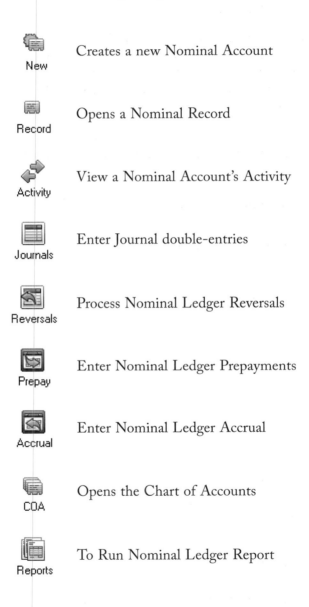

New   Creates a new Nominal Account

Record   Opens a Nominal Record

Activity   View a Nominal Account's Activity

Journals   Enter Journal double-entries

Reversals   Process Nominal Ledger Reversals

Prepay   Enter Nominal Ledger Prepayments

Accrual   Enter Nominal Ledger Accrual

COA   Opens the Chart of Accounts

Reports   To Run Nominal Ledger Report

The Nominal Ledger

The Nominal Ledger, also referred to as the General Ledger, is a grouped analysis of your sales and purchase transactions. For example, when a sales or purchase invoice is posted to the sales or purchase ledger, Sage 50 records it in the Nominal Ledger against the appropriate Nominal account number.

It therefore contains all the accounts for your business, e.g. sales, purchases, expenses, VAT, cash and bank, sundry income, fixed assets, liabilities, capital and owner's drawings. However, it does not keep details of debtors and creditors. These are held in the respective sales and purchase ledgers.

The Nominal accounts let you see quickly where your money is. Information from here is used in the production of management reports to tell you how your business is performing.

1 Click Modules from the menu bar, then Nominal Ledger

2 Select the Ledger view you prefer from these options

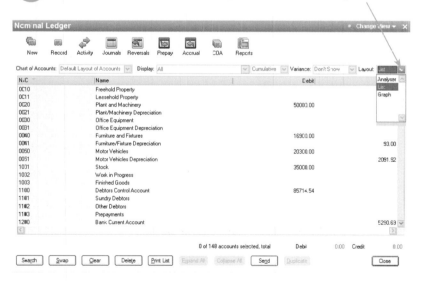

3 Click Close when finished

In Sage 50, you can choose a standard set of nominal accounts during installation, unless in the Startup Wizard you decided to create your own nominal structure. Note that the latter option only creates the Control Accounts for you.

Don't forget

To help you work with the Nominal Ledger, here are some of the standard nominal accounts used by Sage 50:

- Asset Accounts from 0001 to 1999
- Liability Accounts from 2000 to 3999
- Income Accounts from 4000 to 4999
- Purchase Accounts from 5000 to 5999
- Direct Expenses from 6000 to 6999
- Overheads from 7000 to 9999

Hot tip

A shortcut for bringing up the Nominal Ledger window is to click on the following button in the Sage 50 navigation bar:

Nominal Records

You can tailor the nominal accounts to exactly meet your needs by using the Nominal Record window. You have the facility to add, edit and delete nominal accounts as well as viewing transactions posted to each account on a monthly basis.

Using the Record window you can also set budget values for each month of your financial year for a particular nominal account. You can also compare the actual monthly figures against the budget values to keep track of how close you are to meeting targets. To add a nominal account record, do the following:

1 Click Record from the Nominal Ledger to bring up the Nominal Record window

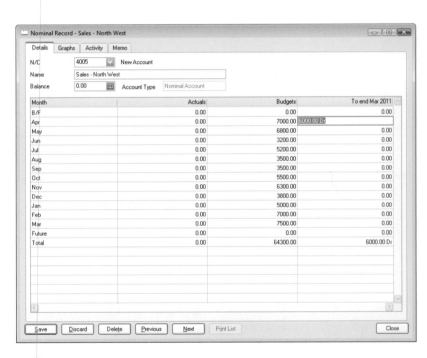

2 In the Details tab box, enter a new nominal account code

3 Press the Tab key and note that this is a New Account

4 Enter new account Name, Budget and Prior Year values

5 Click Save to store details or Discard to start again

Hot tip

Keep track of your business performance by initially entering monthly budget and prior year values, then regularly compare these against the actual values.

Beware

You cannot delete a Nominal Code whilst there is still a balance on it.

Don't forget

The New account details must first be saved before you can enter an Opening Balance.

46

Viewing Nominal Transactions

You can view your Nominal Ledger transactions by using:

- Graphs
- Activity reports
- Table formats

Transaction Analysis using Graphs

A range of 2D and 3D charts is available in Sage 50 to visually compare your current year's trading against the previous year and any budgets you have put in place.

1 From the Nominal Ledger window, select the nominal account you wish to view

2 Click Record, then select the Graphs tab to display data in graphical form

3 To choose a different type of graph, click here, then click on the graph required

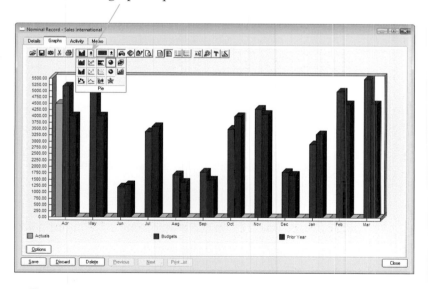

4 Click on the Printer button to print out the graph

5 Click Close to return to the Nominal Ledger window

47

Hot tip

You can save the graph to disk as a chart file. Click on Disk icon and enter a file name.

Hot tip

Include Sage 50 graphs in other documents you may wish to produce by simply using the Camera button to copy the graph, then opening your application and using the paste function to insert it into your other document.

...cont'd

Viewing Nominal Account Activity

You will occasionally need to view transactions that have been posted to the nominal ledger accounts. To do this from the Nominal Ledger window:

1 From the Nominal Ledger window click on the nominal account you wish to view

2 Click on the toolbar Activity button to bring up the Activity window

3 Select a transaction, all items appear in the lower pane

4 Use the scroll bar to move through all the transactions

5 Click on Show to select another range of transactions

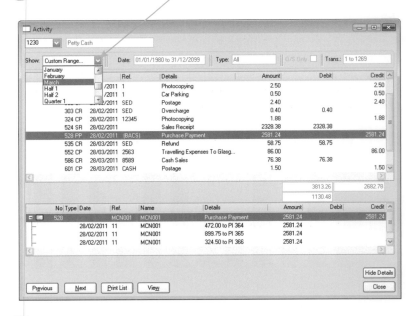

6 Use Previous & Next buttons to view other nominal accounts, if more than one selected in Step 1

7 Click Close to return to the Nominal Ledger

Transaction Codes

Transactions in the Activity window are indicated by a type (Tp) or transaction code, allocated by Sage 50 as follows:

BR (Bank Receipt)	SD (Discount on Sales Receipt)
BP (Bank Payment)	SA (Sales Receipt on Account)
CP (Cash Payment)	PI (Purchase Invoice)
CR (Cash Receipt)	PP (Purchase Payment)
JD (Journal Debit)	PC (Purchase Credit)
JC (Journal Credit)	PD (Discount on Purchase Payment)
SI (Sales Invoice)	PA (Purchase Payment on Account)
SR (Sales Receipt)	VP (Visa Credit Payments)
SC (Sales Credit)	VR (Visa Credit Receipts)

Using Search

It is sometimes handy to reduce the number of records displayed in the Nominal Ledger window or on your reports to only those that match a specific criteria. This will save you having to look through many records for the information needed. For example, to list only control accounts in the Nominal Ledger window:

1 Click Search in the Nominal Ledger window

2 Select Where, choose Account Type Code & Is Equal To

3 Select Control Account from the drop down list

4 Click on the Apply button, then click Close to finish

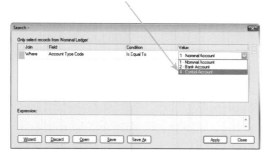

The Journal

The Journal allows you to make transfers between any of your nominal account codes regardless of type (Asset, Liability, Income or Expenditure), provided you adhere to double-entry bookkeeping principles. It lets you enter transactions which may not be covered within the standard Sage 50 facilities.

It is a useful source of reference for these non-regular transactions and can reduce errors by providing a list (audit trail) for checking purposes. Examples of these transactions include correction of errors and transfer of monies, as well as the purchase and sale of fixed assets on credit.

As stated, the Journal follows double-entry bookkeeping principles i.e., the value of the credit transaction must equal the value of the debit transaction. Each line of the Journal Entry table represents a single transaction; therefore there must be at least two transactions in the journal (a credit and a debit).

However, this does not mean that you must post a single credit item for every single debit item. You can, for example, post several debits but only one balancing credit, and vice versa. Provided the net difference between your postings is always zero (i.e. the total value of credits equals the total value of debits), you can then post the Journal.

'Skeleton' Journals

For journals that you make regularly, payments from a bank to a credit card account for example, Sage 50 lets you save the details of that journal entry so that you can use it the next time without having to enter it all again. This is called a 'skeleton'. Some skeleton journals were set up at installation, such as the VAT Liability Transfer Journal.

To save a skeleton journal, click on the Memorise button after you have set up the journal. To load a skeleton journal, click on the Recall button, select the journal you need and click on the Load button. You can even load one of the skeleton journals provided by Sage 50, modify it to suit your needs, then save it.

Reversals

In Sage 50 you can reverse an incorrectly posted journal entry using the Reversals option from the Nominal Ledger window. Use F1 Help for a full explanation of reversing a journal.

Making a Journal Entry

Here is an example of how you would make a journal entry for capital introduced into the business for use in the bank current (1200) and petty cash (1230) accounts.

1. From the Nominal Ledger toolbar, click Journals

2. Use the Calendar button if a different date is required

3. Enter details for both the credit and debit transactions. Reference is optional

4. Note, the default Tax code of T9 is entered for you

5. Check total Debit and Credit are equal and a zero balance is displayed in the Balance box

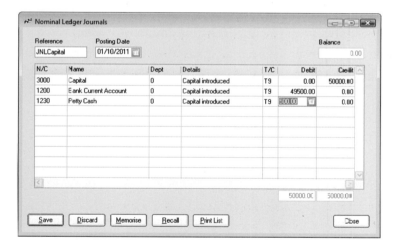

6. To process your journal click Save, or Discard to cancel

7. Click Close to return to Nominal Ledger window

Note that Sage 50 will not automatically calculate VAT or post it to the VAT Control Account. If VAT is required, enter each VAT element as a separate line, with a debit or credit to the appropriate VAT Control Account.

51

Beware

When you make a manual journal entry, VAT is neither calculated for you nor posted to the VAT control account.

Hot tip

If you use a journal entry regularly save it as a Skeleton using the Memorise button, so you can re-create it quickly and easily later.

Memorise

Beware

Before saving the Journal, always ensure the Balance box shows zero. If the value of the credit transactions does not equal the value of the debit transactions, then Sage 50 issues a warning and will not let you save the Journal.

Setting up Prepayments

To adjust statements and reports for any payments which have to be made in advance, for example rent or insurance, there is a Prepayments option available from the Nominal Ledger window. This allows for a payment to be shown as spread over the number of months it refers to, not just the month it was paid in.

After setting up a prepayment, when you run the Month End procedure the correct monthly figure is posted to the appropriate account. All you have to do is to remember to post a suitable payment for the full amount (i.e. from the bank) to the appropriate nominal account.

Hot tip

Just click on the Wizard button to let the Prepayments Wizard guide you through setting up a prepayment:

Wizard

Hot tip

Use Key F6 to save time and reduce errors when copying data from a previous entry.

1. From the Nominal Ledger toolbar, click Prepay to bring up the Prepayments window

2. Enter relevant nominal account code or use Finder button

3. Enter Details, Net Value of prepayment and number of Months prepayment covers (maximum of twelve)

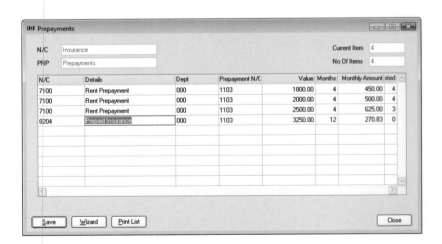

N/C	Details	Dept	Prepayment N/C	Value	Months	Monthly Amount	sted
7100	Rent Prepayment	000	1103	1800.00	4	450.00	4
7100	Rent Prepayment	000	1103	2000.00	4	500.00	4
7100	Rent Prepayment	000	1103	2500.00	4	625.00	3
8204	Prepaid Insurance	000	1103	3250.00	12	270.83	0

N/C: Insurance PRP: Prepayments Current Item: 4 No Of Items: 4

Save Wizard Print List Close

4. Note that the monthly rate is entered for you

5. Click Save to accept prepayment details

6. Click Close to return to Nominal Ledger window

Don't forget

No accounting takes place when prepayment details are saved. Journal Entry postings are only made when the Month End, Post Prepayments option is run.

Setting up Accruals

The Accruals option allows the accounts to be adjusted for any payments you make in one accounting period which in fact relate to a previous period, such as a gas or electricity bill.

In this example, the transaction would be entered using the Accrual and Gas or Electricity accounts. When the charges actually fall due and the bill is paid, the payment transaction is applied to the Accrual account, not the Gas or Electricity account.

As with the prepayments option, the accruals are posted as part of your month end procedure using the Period End, Month End option. This procedure automatically updates the audit trail and nominal accounts records.

1. From the Nominal Ledger window click Accrual

2. Enter nominal account code, or use the Finder button

3. Enter Details, the estimated total Net Value of accrual and number of Months for the accrual

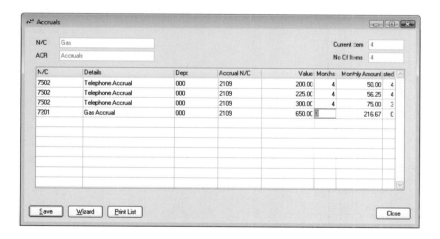

N/C	Details	Dept	Accrual N/C	Value	Months	Monthly Amount	sted
7502	Telephone Accrual	000	2109	200.00	4	50.00	4
7502	Telephone Accrual	000	2109	225.00	4	56.25	4
7502	Telephone Accrual	000	2109	300.00	4	75.00	3
7201	Gas Accrual	000	2109	650.00	3	216.67	0

4. Monthly accrual is calculated for you

5. Click Save to accept accrual details

6. Click Close to return to Nominal Ledger window

Hot tip

The Post column shows how many postings have been made using the Month End Post prepayment option.

Don't forget

No accounting takes place when accrual details are saved. Journal Entry postings are only made when the Month End, Post Accruals option is run.

Hot tip

If you have already set up some Accrual entries, these appear in the Accruals window when it opens. Just add your new Accrual at the end of the list.

The Chart of Accounts

During installation, Sage 50 created a simple Chart of Accounts suitable for standard reporting, such as Profit and Loss, Balance Sheet, Budget and Prior Year Reports.

It may be that the default account names are not suitable for your business, so the Chart of Accounts can be customised to meet your business requirements. New category types can be introduced into the accounts or current categories edited to reflect, for example, the actual items sold within your business.

Don't forget

The chart of Accounts is subdivided into the following default report category types:

Profit & Loss
- Sales
- Purchases
- Direct Expenses
- Overheads

Balance Sheet
- Fixed Assets
- Current Assets
- Current Liabilities
- Long Term Liabilities
- Capital & Reserves

1   To examine the Chart of Accounts' facilities, click COA from the Nominal Ledger window

2   If you want to look at a chart, select it from the list and click Edit

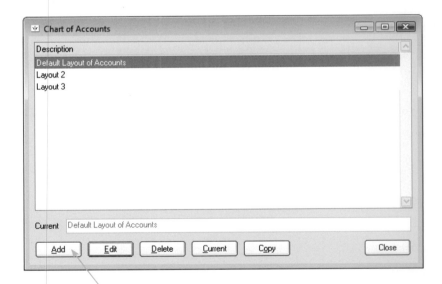

3   To create a new Chart of Accounts, click the Add button

Don't forget

Always check that the name of the layout you selected appears automatically in the 'Current' text box.

4   To use a particular Chart of Accounts simply highlight it from the list and click the Current button

5   When finished, click Close to return to the Nominal Ledger window

Creating a Chart of Accounts Layout

Do the following to add a new Chart of Accounts layout:

1 Click COA from the Nominal Ledger window

2 Click Add in the Chart of Accounts window

3 Enter name of your new Chart of Accounts layout

4 Click Add
to continue

5 Click on a category and change its description to that required in your financial reports

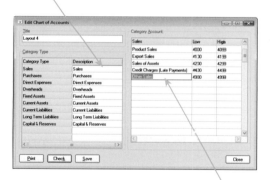

6 Enter (or amend) the headings for each range of nominal accounts in the selected category and set range of nominal accounts to be included for each selected category in Low & High boxes

7 Click Check to see if you've made any errors then click Save, or Close to discard

8 To print your Chart of Accounts, click Print, then Run

Don't forget

If you elected to create your own chart of accounts during the Startup Wizard, the default chart of accounts will not contain any category accounts.

Hot tip

Use the Check button to quickly find any nominal account errors in your new layout.

Nominal Reports

To print or preview reports using the nominal data already entered into the system, use the Reports option from the Nominal Ledger. Sage 50 already supplies a considerable number of pre-installed reports to suit most needs, but you can create additional custom reports using the all new Report Designer. See Chapter 12 for more details on creating reports.

To print a Nominal Ledger report, do the following:

1 From the Nominal Ledger toolbar, click Reports

2 Click on folder & select report layout required

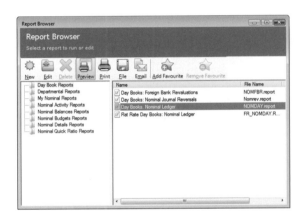

3 Click the Preview button to begin generating the report

4 Type range details or use Calendar and Finder buttons

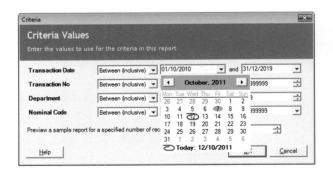

5 Click OK to preview report

5 The Bank

This chapter shows you how to maintain your bank account records and transactions. This includes deposits, payments, transfer of money between bank accounts and adjustments to show bank charges and interest received. It also covers reconciling your statements, processing recurring entries and the production of cheques.

58 The Bank Toolbar

59 Bank Accounts

60 Bank, Cash & Credit Accounts

61 Recording Bank Payments

62 Supplier Invoice Payments

63 Batch Purchase Payments

64 Bank Receipts

65 Recording Customer Receipts

66 Bank Transfers

67 Recurring Entries

68 Generating Cheques

69 The Bank Statement

70 Bank Account Reconciliation

72 Bank Reports

The Bank Toolbar

This toolbar provides features for the recording and maintenance of bank transactions and records. You can perform adjustments, record the transfer of monies, enter receipts, produce statements and reports and even print cheques.

Hot tip

To quickly create a new Bank account, use the New Wizard from the Bank Toolbar and work through the simple step by step screens.

New

58

Record
Opens a Bank Record

Reconcile
Opens Bank Account Reconciliation

Payment
Record Bank Payments

Supplier
Record Supplier Payments

Remittance
To Print Bank Remittances

Batch
To Record a Batch Purchase Payment

Receipt
Record Money Received

Customer
Record Customer Receipts

Transfer
Make Bank Transfers

Recurring
Opens Recurring Entries Window

Cash Flow
Opens the Cash Flow Window

Statement
To Print Bank Statements

Cheques
To Print Cheques

Reports
To Run Bank Account Reports

Bank Accounts

There are three types of Bank accounts used in Sage 50: the Bank Account, Cash Account and Credit Card Account.

The Bank account option treats both Bank and Building Societies as bank accounts. Three bank accounts have been automatically set up to include a bank current account, a bank deposit account and a building society account.

A single Cash Account called Petty Cash has been set up, but other cash accounts can be added, for example, Emergency Cash or Additional Travel Expenses etc.

The facility to record your credit card bank details is available and allows you to monitor any credit card transactions you have made and keep track of your money. A Company Credit Card account has already been set up for use.

To view the Bank account window:

Don't forget

Remember to have your current bank balance to hand when creating new Bank records.

1 Select Bank from the Sage 50 navigation bar

2 Click on the bank account required, then click on the appropriate icon for the function you wish to carry out

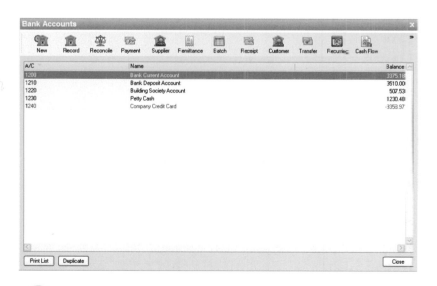

3 When finished, click Close

Bank, Cash & Credit Accounts

Sage 50 provides three types of bank accounts:

- Bank Account (includes both bank deposit and current account, plus a building society account).

- Cash Account (named Petty Cash).

- Credit Card Account (company credit card and credit card receipts).

These accounts can be edited to match your own details. Accounts can also be added or deleted. To set up your Bank account details:

1 From the Bank Accounts window, select account type required and click on the Record icon

2 Check details and make changes if necessary

3 Click here to enter Current Balance

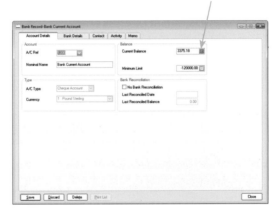

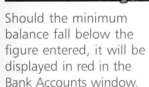
4 Enter Opening Balance and other details then click Save

5 Click Bank Details tab and enter any further relevant details

6 Click Save to store details, then Close

Recording Bank Payments

For recording any non-invoiced or one-off payments use the Payment option from the Bank Accounts window. Sage 50 then makes it very easy for you to keep track of where your money goes – simply select the appropriate account, enter the payment and post it.

To record Bank payments:

1 Click Payment from the Bank Accounts window

2 Use Finder button to enter Bank account code

3 Enter Date (and transaction Reference if required)

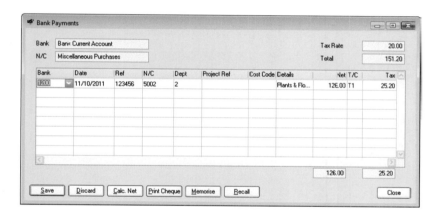

Bank	Date	Ref	N/C	Dept	Project Ref	Cost Code	Details	Net	T/C	Tax
1200	11/10/2011	123456	5002	2			Plants & Flo...	126.00	T1	25.20
								126.00		25.20

Bank: Bank Current Account
N/C: Miscellaneous Purchases
Tax Rate: 20.00
Total: 151.20

Save Discard Calc. Net Print Cheque Memorise Recall Close

4 Enter a Nominal Code for the payment to be posted to, or use the Finder button

5 Enter Details describing the payment

6 Enter the amount (change Tax Code from default of T1 if necessary)

7 Click Save to post details (update the nominal ledger and the Bank account)

8 Click Close to return to the Bank Accounts window

Hot tip

Payments to your suppliers should be entered using the Supplier option as this brings up any outstanding invoices when the supplier account is entered.

Hot tip

If you only know the Gross value of the payment, simply enter it in the Net box and click on the Calc. Net button.

Hot tip

Use the Discard button if you want to clear any data already entered and start again. Any entries you have already saved will not be cancelled.

Supplier Invoice Payments

The Supplier option from the Bank Accounts toolbar will provide you with a detailed transaction list of any outstanding invoice items, credit notes and payments made on account to suppliers. To record payment of a supplier invoice do the following:

1 In the Bank Accounts window, select the account required (e.g. Bank Current Account) & click the Supplier button

2 Enter supplier account code in the Payee field

3 Use Calendar button if payment date is different

4 Enter cheque number if required (See the first DON'T FORGET icon in the margin)

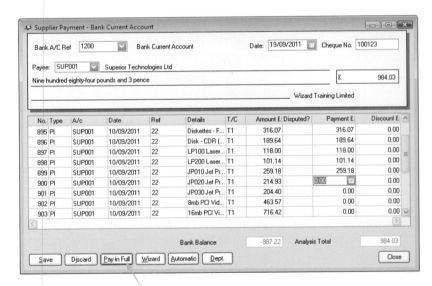

5 Enter value in Payment box for part-payment or click on Pay in Full button to enter full amount

6 Repeat Step 5 for any remaining transactions

7 Click Save to save payment details, then Close to return to the Bank Accounts wondow

Batch Purchase Payments

You can list all outstanding purchase invoices, purchase credit
notes and purchase payments on account for all suppliers
using the Batch option from the Bank Accounts window. The
transactions are sorted in order, firstly by supplier and then by
transaction number.

Outstanding transactions can be paid in three ways:

- All transactions paid in full
- Individual transactions paid in full
- Individual transactions paid in part

To record full or part payments:

1 From Bank Accounts select the account and click Batch

2 To pay ALL outstanding transactions click Pay All

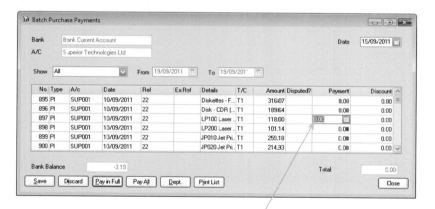

3 To make INDIVIDUAL full payments, select a
transaction and click on the Pay in Full button

4 For a PART PAYMENT simply enter the amount in the
Payment box

5 When finished click Save, or Discard to start again

6 Click Close

Hot tip

You can pay a
transaction either in full
or part.

Don't forget

All outstanding
transactions can be paid
in full in one go using
the Pay All button, but
note that there will only
be one posting.

63

Don't forget

If any of the selected
transactions are in
dispute Sage 50 displays
a warning message.

Bank Receipts

To record any non-invoiced or miscellaneous payments you receive, the Receipts option from the Bank Accounts window is used. These items are allocated a specific nominal code for analysis purposes so a check can be made on monies received.

To enter receipt of money:

Hot tip

If you only have the Gross value to hand, enter it in the Net box and click on Calc. Net.

1 From the Bank Account window click the Receipt icon

2 In Bank Receipts select the appropriate Bank account

3 Ensure the required Date is entered

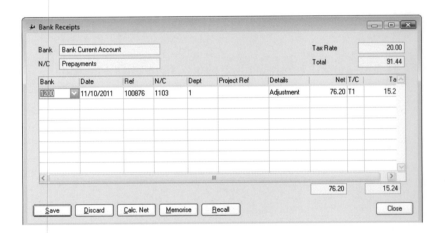

4 Enter a suitable Reference, such as a cheque number

Hot tip

A receipt reference, i.e. cheque number or deposit number, will help you when reconciling bank accounts.

5 Select a Nominal Account Code to post the receipt to and give Details

6 Enter the Net value

7 Repeat Steps 2–6 to record further receipts, then click Save to post transactions

8 When finished, Close all windows

Recording Customer Receipts

The Customer option from the Bank Accounts window is used to record money received from your customers. When the customer's account reference is entered, any outstanding invoices appear automatically in the Customer Receipt window.

To record full or part payments:

1 From the Bank Accounts window, select the bank account required and click Customer

2 Enter a customer Account Code to display all items not fully paid for that customer

3 Check Date and enter a paying in Reference, if possible

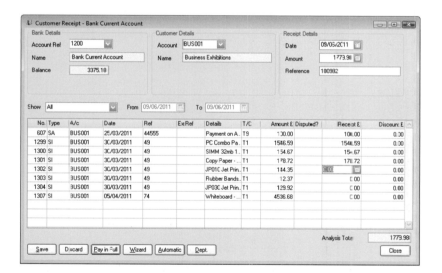

4 If FULL payment has been received select a transaction and click Pay in Full

5 If this is a PART payment enter the amount received

6 Enter any further receipts then click Save to process them

7 When finished, Close all windows

Don't forget

You can pay an invoice in full or part but you cannot allocate an amount more than the item value.

Hot tip

Use the Customers Receipt Wizard to help you record any cheques received for customer invoice payments, allocate credit notes and payments on account to invoices or to just post a payment on account.

65

Don't forget

Sage 50 automatically warns you of any disputed items.

Bank Transfers

Sometimes you will need to transfer money from one bank account to another. You can record this using the Transfer option from the Bank Accounts window or by making a journal entry.

To make a bank transfer do the following:

1 From the Bank Accounts window, select the bank you wish to move the money from

2 Click Transfer to open the Bank Transfer window

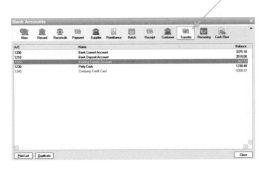

3 Enter Nominal Code of the Bank you are transferring to

4 Enter a Reference and appropriate Details

5 Check the date in the Date box & enter transfer amount

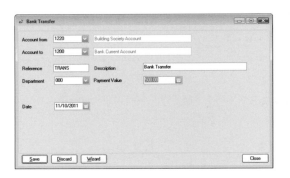

6 Click Save to process or Discard to start again

7 Click Close to finish, then Close again

Recurring Entries

For payments which remain consistent and are paid on a monthly basis, for example rent and electricity, the Recurring option can be used from the Bank Accounts window. This feature is also useful for standing orders and direct debits and prevents payments such as these from being overlooked. Each month, these transactions need posting to update your banks and ledgers.

If there are any outstanding recurring entries, Sage 50 reminds you on startup and asks if you wish to post them. To add a recurring entry:

1 Select Recurring from the Bank Accounts window and Click Add

2 Enter transaction type from the list box

3 Enter the Bank Account Code

4 Enter a Nominal Code to post the transaction to

5 Give Reference & Details, then enter Posting Frequency data

6 Enter Net amount and check the Tax Code

7 Click OK to return to the Recurring Entries window

8 Click Process and Process All to process the recurring entries, then click Close to finish

Beware

Note that recurring entries need processing each month before you can run the Month or Year End procedures.

Don't forget

Sage 50 will only let you post journal credits when you post journal debits of the same value, and vice versa.

67

Don't forget

The Last Posted box always remains blank until the new entry is saved and processed.

Hot tip

If you need to stop a monthly payment simply click the Suspend Posting box. This is handy for those payments which do not need posting every month.

Add / Edit Recurring Entry

Transaction Type: Bank/Cash/Credit Card Payment

Recurring Entry From / To
Bank A/C: 1200 — Bank Current Account
Nominal Code: 0030 — Office Equipment

Recurring Entry Details
Transaction Ref: DD/STO
Transaction Details: Office Furniture Lease
Department: 0

Posting Frequency
Every: 1 Month(s) Total Required Postings: 24
Start Date: 05/11/2011 Finish Date: 05/10/2013
Next Posting Date: 05/11/2011 Suspend Posting ?: ☐
Last Posted:

Posting Amounts
Net Amount: 60.00 Tax Code: T1 20.00 VAT: 12.00

OK Cancel

Generating Cheques

This feature provides you with the ability to print cheques automatically for a particular bank account. All Purchase Payments (type PP) and Purchase Payments on Account (type PA) transactions not previously printed and with blank references are listed in the Print Cheques window. This is how to print cheques using the cheque generator:

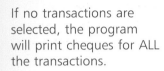
1 From the Bank Accounts window, select the required bank account and click on the Cheques button

2 Allocate a new Cheque Number if required

3 Select transactions requiring cheques

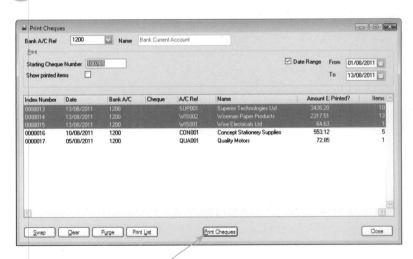

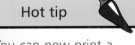

Hot tip

You can now print a cheque for a supplier without first having to set up an account.

4 Click Print Cheques

5 Select layout required, then click Run

6 Click Yes if cheques printed correctly, then Close

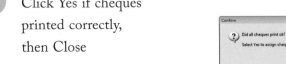

The Bank Statement

Sage 50 provides you with the facility to print your bank statements out at any time, showing all reconciled bank payments and receipts. These statements show the transactions made to and from each bank account, and prove useful for cross-referencing purposes when checking for any transaction omissions or additions. To print a report in bank statement format:

1 From the Bank Accounts window select the desired account and click on Statement

2 Select Preview from Output options and Click Run

3 Enter Transaction Date range here and click OK to preview

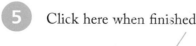

4 Click Print, then OK from the print dialog box

5 Click here when finished

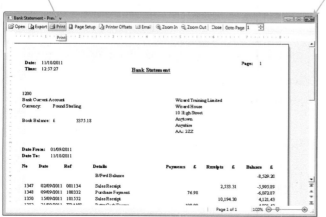

Don't forget

To use this facility effectively, make sure that you enter all Bank transactions accurately and completely so that the Sage 50 Bank statements match your actual bank statements.

Hot tip

You can also save the Bank Statement reports as a file for use at a later date. Simply click on the Save As button in the report preview window.

Hot tip

To bring up previously saved statements, click Open and select the required statement from the list.

Bank Account Reconciliation

Bank reconciliation is the process of matching up your computer bank records and transactions with those shown on the statements received from your bank.

The Bank Reconciliation window displays transactions which have not been previously reconciled. After entering the date of the statement, you can work through your bank statement matching the transactions recorded in Sage 50. If necessary, you should make any adjustments needed to ensure that Sage 50 bank accounts accurately reflect the transactions processed by your actual bank. To reconcile a bank account:

Don't forget

Before you select any transactions to reconcile, always check that the opening balance shown in the Bank Reconciliation window is the same as the opening balance on your actual bank statement.

1 From the Bank Accounts window select the bank account to be reconciled, then click Reconcile

2 Enter the closing balance of your bank statement

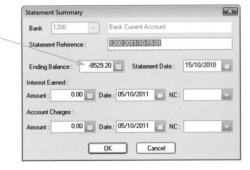

3 Enter date of the bank statement, complete details, then Click OK

4 Click each transaction that matches the bank statement

5 Click Match button to add transactions to lower pane

Beware

A bank account cannot be reconciled if the check box No Bank Reconciliation is ticked on the bank record.

6 Check that the Reconcile and Statement End balances match, then click Save

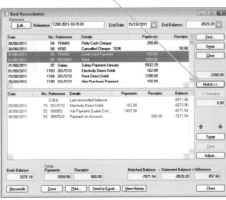

7 Click Close

Bank reconciliation will only work correctly provided that a number of important rules are followed:

- The opening balance shown on the Bank Reconciliation window must match the opening balance on your actual bank statement

If for some reason they are different, you will need to check why and make the necessary adjustments. One way of doing this is to view the selected bank's activity from within the nominal ledger. To see if a transaction is reconciled, check the Bank column in the Audit Trail, where: R = reconciled and N = not reconciled.

- Work through your actual bank statement progressively one line at a time, clicking on the corresponding transaction entry in the Bank reconciliation window to highlight it

- If you come across a transaction on your bank statement not shown in Sage 50, you should record this transaction immediately using the Adjustments facility

- Check everything carefully. When you are satisfied that all transactions for reconciliation have been selected and any adjustments made, the Difference box should show zero

Making Adjustments

1 From the Reconciliation window, click the Add Adjustment button

2 Enter the Nominal Code of the account to receive the adjustment

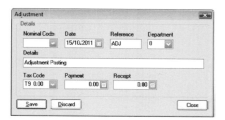

3 Enter adjustment details and value

4 If correct click Save, then Close

Bank Reports

There is a wide range of ready-to-use bank reports provided by Sage 50. These reports outline your bank details and transactions and help you keep track of your bank finances. It is advisable that you regularly print out the standard reports, such as Day Books, once you have entered the relevant transactions.

1 From the Bank Accounts window, click Reports to bring up the Bank Reports window

2 Click on a folder and select the report required

3 Click on Preview button

4 Enter any Criteria if required, click OK then Print

Cash Flow Window

A useful feature in Sage 50 is the cash flow display, showing outstanding payments, receipts and recurring entries.

1 From the toolbar click the Cash Flow button

2 Click Print if required

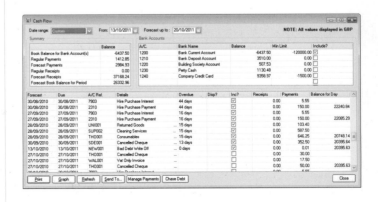

6 Products

Learn how to create and maintain records for the products you buy and sell and how to set up product codes. You will also see how to monitor stock levels, the movement of stock and how to analyse product transactions.

74 The Products Toolbar

75 The Product Record

78 Product Defaults

79 Using Search

80 Bill of Materials

81 Viewing Transactions

82 Product Activity

84 Product Adjustments

85 Product Transfers

86 Product Reports

The Products Toolbar

The Products toolbar provides features for the recording and maintenance of product records and transactions. You have the facility to record the movement of your products and make any adjustments and/or transfer of stock. Product activity can be analysed and reports generated.

Record   Opens a Product Record

Prices   To Set up a Price List

Activity   View a Product Activity

Shortfall   To Run the Product Shortfall Generator

In   Make Stock In Adjustments

Out   Make Stock Out Adjustments

Transfer   Record Stock Transfers

Stk Take   Automatically Make Stock Adjustments

Chk BOM   Check Make-Up Capability For Stock

Returns   For Recording Stock Returns

Allocate   For Recording Stock Allocations

Labels   To Produce Product Labels

Reports   To Run Product Report

The Product Record

Sage 50 allows you to create, edit or delete records for all the products your business sells. Once these records have been set up all you need to do is enter a product code and the details will be automatically included for you on any product invoice, credit note or order you create.

From the Product Record window you can view the sales price and quantity in stock for each product. Use the Products option to:

- Create and maintain records for all products bought or sold

- Record product movements

- Analyse product transactions using tables or graphs

- Set up a Bill of Materials

- Keep track of your stock levels

From the Product Record window you can view the Sales Price and Quantity in stock for each product, together with the Product Code and Description.

1. Select Products from the Sage 50 navigation bar

2. To view Product details, select a product and click on Record

3. To finish click Close

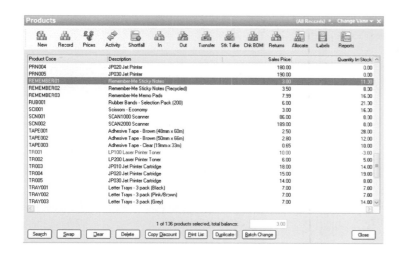

Don't forget

Opening Balances need setting up for your products. Follow the same procedures as for your customers, suppliers, nominal and bank accounts.

Beware

Once a product record has been set up, take care before deleting it, even if there is zero stock and no more is expected. It may still belong to a part allocated order.

75

Don't forget

Use the Stock Take option to make adjustments to your stock levels after you have completed a stock take. All you need to do is enter the current stock levels for your products and Sage 50 makes all of the necessary adjustments for you.

...cont'd

Entering a product record

Hot tip

You can update the sales price for all product items using the Global Changes option from the Tools menu.

Beware

If the Ignore Stock Levels check box is selected (ticked) on the product record, its details will not appear on some reports, i.e. Stock History.

Don't forget

You can save your stock take details to a file for opening at a later date, to continue with the stock take, or to view the adjustments that you previously made. Remember, however, to enter all of your stock take details before you process any transactions that would alter your stock levels. This is because your stock details may change between the date that the last stock date was saved and the next time it is re-opened.

1 From the Products window click on Record

2 Type a unique Product Code and press Tab

3 Enter Description, check the Nominal sales & VAT code

4 Enter Sales Price here

5 Click on O/B button then Yes to save changes

6 Check for correct Date & enter Quantity

7 Enter Cost Price of the Product

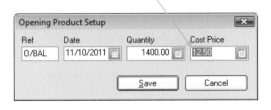

8 Click Save, then Close to return to the Products window

Entering details onto the Product Record

Whilst the Product Record has been designed to accept a considerable amount of detail, not every item is applicable to all products. However, to make reporting more accurate later, you should try and include as much detail as possible about a product when adding records.

Not all of the boxes on the Product Record will accept user entry though. Sage 50 calculates or generates the following information and enters it for you. It cannot be directly edited.

Allocated
This figure shows the quantity of the product which has been partly or fully allocated on the sales order, but which has not yet been despatched.

Free Stock
Sage 50 calculates the Free Stock as being the In Stock total minus the Allocated stock total.

On Order
Using the Purchase Orders option, this is the quantity of the product which has been put 'on order'.

Last Ord Qty
This shows the amount of stock ordered when the last purchase order for this product was put 'on order'.

Last Ord Date
This shows the date of the last purchase order raised for this product after being put on order.

Cost Price
This is the latest cost price for the product item, entered using the Opening Balance option, the Adjustments In option, Purchase Order Processing or the Global Changes option (useful for updating cost prices for all or selected product items).

When running financial or management reports, you must remember that Sage 50 will use this latest price even though products already in stock may have actually cost more or less. This may, on occasion, give distorted figures, such as when calculating the total cost value of a product item in stock.

Hot tip

If stock level falls below the re-order level, the item appears red in the Products window and also appears on the Re-order report.

Hot tip

If you use or propose to use a bar code reader, enter the bar code character string in the product details section of the Product Record.

Beware

If you do not enter a Cost Price in the Opening Product Setup box, the product cost is recorded as zero. This could affect some of your finance reports later.

Product Defaults

To save entering repetitive details and to make the process of creating new product records easier, Sage 50 includes the facility to set up various product defaults.

Whenever a new product record is created, certain regular details, e.g. Nominal Code, Tax Code, Department etc, are asked for. If you use a recording system where these codes remain the same for most of your products, default settings can be set up which will then appear automatically in each new product record without you having to enter them every time. To set up product defaults:

Don't forget

If you set the Unit DP to a value greater than 2, the net amount on any product invoice created will still be rounded to 2 decimal places.

1 From the Sage 50 menu bar, first select Settings, then Product Defaults

2 Enter the Nominal Code to be used by default whenever you create orders and product invoices

3 Select the VAT rate & Purchase code, if relevant

4 Enter Unit of Sale, e.g. 'each' or 'box', then choose Category and Department as required

5 Enter number of decimal places for Quantity and Unit sale price

6 Click OK to save or Cancel to discard any changes

Hot tip

You can use the Descriptions tab to quickly set up your own product discount names.

Using Search

Using Search speeds up the process of searching for specific product records, for example to show products which match a particular description, or those below the re-order stock level. The following example shows how to set up a search to restrict Product Records to only those with less than 50 in stock:

1 Click the Search button in the bottom left hand corner of the Products window to bring up the Search window

2 Click Where in the first column

3 Select Quantity in stock in this field

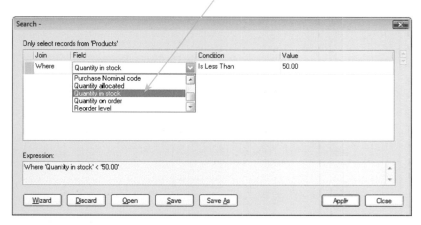

4 Select Is Less Than in the Condition column

5 Enter 50 in the Value field

6 Click Apply & Close to return to the Products window

7 Note that only records matching the search are displayed. The title bar indicates the Search is applied

8 To cancel the search and show all records, click this icon

Hot tip

The calculator button is a quick and handy way of making an entry in the Value field.

Hot tip

Use the Save button to record searches you use frequently. You can then recall these as required from the Search window.

79

Don't forget

Search remains applied to a list until you click the search icon on the right hand side of the title bar:

Bill of Materials

This term relates to a product you hold in stock made up from other products you keep. The made up product is sometimes known as a product assembly and is said to have a Bill of Materials. For example, a first aid kit is a product assembly consisting of various components – bandages, tablets, plasters, etc.

For businesses selling a product made up of other products, it is useful to set up a Bill of Materials. In Sage 50 this feature keeps track of stock levels and can automatically calculate how many products you can make up for sale from the stock you currently hold and at what cost price. To set up a Bill of Materials for a product do the following:

Hot tip

Use the Transfer button from the Products window to increase the stock levels of your product assemblies.

Don't forget

The Bill of Materials table itemises each individual component for the product assembly.

Hot tip

See how many product assemblies you can make up by looking in the Available to Makeup box.

1 From the Products window, select the product you wish to set up a Bill of Materials for, then click Record

2 Click the BOM tab from the Product Record

3 Enter Product Code for each item

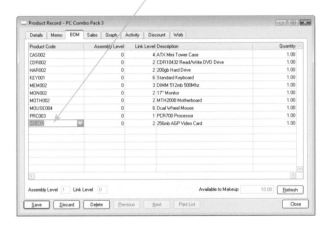

4 Enter quantity required for product assembly

5 Click Refresh to see how many you can make from stock

6 Click Save to store, or Discard to start again

7 Click Close

Viewing Transactions

The Sales Tab

You can use this dialog box to view the sales value and quantity sold for your selected product during the financial year on a month by month basis. With a record selected:

1 From the Product Record click on the Sales tab

2 Click Close when finished

Hot tip

To amend values for all, or a selected group of products within the Product Record, use the Global Changes option from the Tools menu.

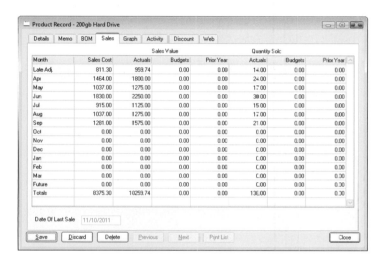

Hot tip

Use a range of 2D and 3D chart types to compare how you did last year compared to this year's budgets.

Product Discounts

1 From the Product Record click on the Discount tab

2 Enter quantities for customer to qualify for a discount & % Discount

3 Discounted value is calculated for you

4 Click Save, then Close

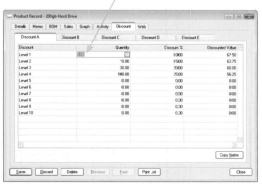

Hot tip

Use the Copy Matrix button to copy the discount structure from another already discounted product.

Product Activity

Details regarding adjustments of goods in and out, stock transfers, current quantities in stock, on order and allocated prove invaluable when trying to fulfil orders or analyse and track stock movement.

You can decide when you no longer wish to retain certain transactions on your system by using the Clear Stock option. This facility enables transactions to be cleared from your Product History prior to a specific date.

It is important that you understand the following terms when trying to calculate the availability of stock and to understand the product reports produced by Sage 50:

Tp: A code to identify the type of transaction, where:

AI	=	Adjustment In
AO	=	Adjustment Out
MI	=	Movement In (product transfer only)
MO	=	Movement Out (product transfer only)
GR	=	Goods Returned (via credit notes)
GO	=	Goods Out (via sales orders and product invoices)
GI	=	Goods In (via purchase orders)
DI	=	Damages In
DO	=	Damages Out
WO	=	Write Off

Used: This is the sum of all the AO (Adjustments Out), GO (Goods Out) and MO (Movements Out) quantities for the product within the specified date range.

Cost: If the transaction line refers to an AI (Adjustment In), GI (Goods In), GR (Goods Returned) or MI (Movement In), this shows the cost price.

Sale: Where a transaction line refers to an AO (Adjustment Out), GO (Goods Out) or GR (Goods Returned), this shows the sales price.

Qty on Order: This is the product quantity which has been placed on order using the Purchase Order option, but not yet delivered.

Qty Allocated: This shows the product quantity that has been allocated to sales orders using the Sales Order Processing option.

Qty in Stock: This is the sum of all the AI (Adjustments In), MI (Movements In), GI (Goods In) and GR (Goods Received), less the quantity used for the specified period.

Qty Available: The Quantity in Stock less Quantity Allocated.

To view Activity from the Products window:

1 Click on the product or products required

2 From the Products toolbar click the Activity button

3 Click here to select a diferent Date Range

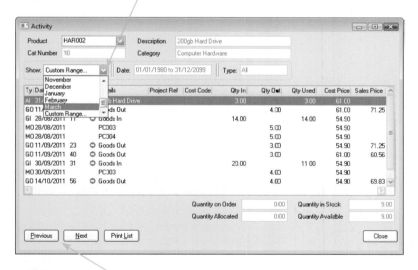

4 Click Previous or Next if more than one product selected

5 Click Close when finished

Hot tip

Viewing a product's activity is also available using the Activity tab from within the Product Record window.

Hot tip

Use the Transaction Type range facility in the Date Range window to refine and speed up your search of Product activity.

83

Hot tip

Use the Finder button to select another Product Code if required.

Product Adjustments

The In and Out options from the Product window are used to record adjustments to your product's stock levels, such as when stock is received into stores, an order is returned, or stock is taken out as damaged.

The In button is used to enter any increase in a product's available stock, whilst the Out option is for recording a decrease.

To make Adjustments In

Hot tip

If there is a discrepancy after a stock take, just enter the stock adjustment using the Stock Take option.

1 From the Products window click the In option

2 Enter Product Code, Date & Ref, Quantity in and enter the new Cost if changed

Don't forget

Cost prices are important to the valuation of the stock as product levels are controlled on a first in, first out basis. Always enter cost prices, therefore, to achieve accurate valuation.

3 Click Save to store changes and Close

The Out button is used to record any miscellaneous product movements which decrease a product's available stock level and where no product invoice has been raised.

To make Adjustments Out

Beware

You cannot use the Returns option for non-stock or service items.

1 Click on Out

2 Enter the Product Code and Quantity, then click Save

84

Product Transfers

This feature is used for increasing the In Stock quantity of Product Assemblies using components currently in stock. The Product Assemblies are set up using the Bill of Materials option (see page 80).

When using the Stock Transfers option the cost price for each Product Assembly is calculated for you by Sage 50, by adding together the cost price of each component.

To make a product transfer from the Products window:

1 Click on the Transfer button

2 Click on the Product Code Finder button

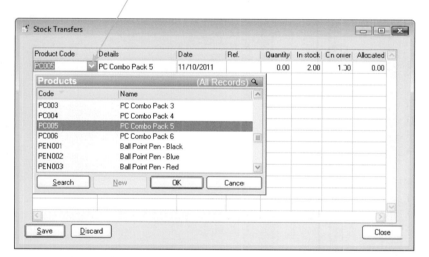

3 Select the desired Product Assembly Code & click OK

4 Check Details and Date

5 Enter Quantity required, Sage 50 warns you if insufficient stock available to make the product assembly

6 Click Save to record entries or Discard to start again

7 Click Close

Beware

You can only use a product code which has been previously set up to be a product assembly using the BOM option.

Don't forget

If you do not have sufficient stock of components to make up the quantity you have entered, Sage 50 will display a warning.

Hot tip

Quickly check your component stock levels by clicking on the Shortfall button on the Products toolbar to bring up the Shortfall Generator window (Accounts Plus and Professional only).

Shortfall

Hot tip

Use Check BOM to quickly check which stock items and components are needed to complete orders.

Product Reports

The Stock Reports option allows you to print out a wide range of useful pre-prepared product related reports. These reports show such things as product details and movements, and will help you to keep track of what you have in stock, its financial value etc.

Additional product reports tailored to your business needs can be created using the Report Designer (See Chapter 12). To run a Product Report:

1 From the Products window click Reports

2 First click on the required folder and select a report

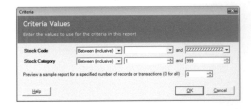

3 Click Preview button to generate report

4 Enter any required Criteria

5 Click OK to generate report

6 Click Print, then Close when done

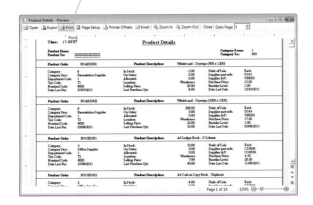

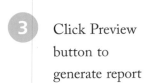

7 Invoices

This chapter shows you how to produce invoices and credit notes for your products and services. Customers, Products and Nominal Accounts are directly linked to Invoicing so the invoices produced automatically update the relevant ledgers.

88	The Invoicing Toolbar
89	Invoicing
90	The Product Invoice
92	Printing an Invoice
93	The Service Invoice
95	The Skeleton Invoice
96	Product Credit Note
97	Process Recurring Transactions
98	Updating your Ledgers
99	Printing for Batch Invoicing
100	Producing Reports

The Invoicing Toolbar

This toolbar provides facilities for generating invoices, quotes, proformas and credit notes for the goods you sell and the services you provide. Ledgers can be automatically updated, transactions printed out and reports generated for analysis.

 New/Edit   To Create or View an Invoice, Pro-forma or Credit Note

 Recurring   To Open Saved Skeleton or Recurring Transactions

 Print   To Print an Invoice or a Credit Note

 Email   To Email Invoices

 Update   To Update Ledgers

 Labels   To Print Invoice Labels

 Reports   To Run Invoicing Reports

Invoicing

Processing manually generated invoices, or batch invoicing, i.e. items not generated using Sage 50, has already been referred to in Chapters 2 and 3. Briefly, Chapter 2 (Customers) explains how to log invoices and credit notes within the system after they have been produced and sent to customers. Chapter 3 (Suppliers) explains how to record the invoices and credit notes you receive from your suppliers.

Invoicing deals with Sage 50 generated invoices, of which there are two basic types. First there is the Product Invoice, which is used for invoicing customers for the products you sell. Each line of the invoice can be used for recording specific product items. Early discount settlement can be offered on these invoices and carriage charges applied.

Meanwhile, the Service Invoice is used to invoice customers you have provided a service for. An unlimited amount of text can be entered into the invoice describing the services supplied. Discount settlement can be applied and carriage charges recorded.

As Sage 50 generates these invoices, all the relevant details are automatically recorded and posted for you when you are ready. For invoices where the same information is entered regularly, the Memorise option saves the invoice as a template. This template can then be recalled when required and updated with the new information, saving valuable time.

Within Invoicing is the facility to generate credit notes for your customers, where products or services for example, have not been received or had to be returned. When these transactions are posted, the ledgers will be updated automatically.

You do, of course, need to keep track of your invoicing. Use the report facility regularly to print out a list of Invoices not yet printed or posted, or to check on stock requirements or shortfalls for the invoices you have generated using this Invoicing option.

In older versions of Sage 50, the Invoicing toolbar contained separate buttons for Product and Service Invoices and Credit Notes. With newer versions the toolbar contains only one New/Edit button. The type of Invoice or Credit Note is then selected from the Type and Format boxes in the Invoice window.

Don't forget

Sage 50 generates invoice numbers in sequence, normally starting at 1. However, you can start with your own numbering system, of up to seven digits. This will be incremented for you each time a new invoice is generated.

Don't forget

Your invoices remain in the Invoicing window list box until removed using the Delete option.

The Product Invoice

Beware

You cannot amend a product invoice where the quantity was entered using the Sales Order Processing option.

Hot tip

Provided the appropriate cost details have been entered on the Product records, use the Profit button to quickly calculate how much profit an Invoice makes.

Don't forget

As well as normal product codes, you can also enter special non-product codes:

S1 = Special product item with price and VAT amount

S2 = Special product item, exempt for VAT (Tax code T0)

S3 = Special service item with price and VAT amount

M = Message, with a description and up to two comment lines

To invoice your customers for the products you sell, use the New/Edit option from the Invoicing toolbar, then select the Product option in the drop down list in the Type box. To create an Invoice click Modules, then Invoicing, from the menu bar and do the following:

1 Click New/Edit on the Invoicing toolbar. Invoice and Product appears in Type & Format by default

2 Enter the tax point date if different

3 Type Sales Order No. if applicable

4 Enter Customer Account Code, Customer details appear

5 Enter the Product Code (use the Finder button), followed by the Quantity

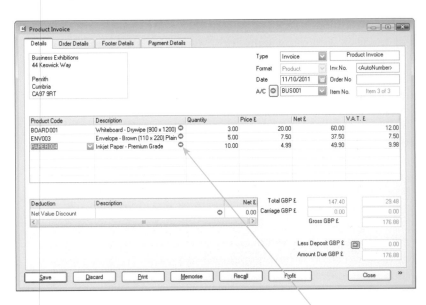

6 Repeat Step 5 for further products, clicking here if you need to edit any of the product details, then click Save

7 Click Close

Product Invoice Order Details

You can also record useful additional Order Details on your Invoice if necessary:

1 Click on Order Details tab

2 Enter Delivery Address and any Notes if required

3 Enter Customer Order Details, especially Order No

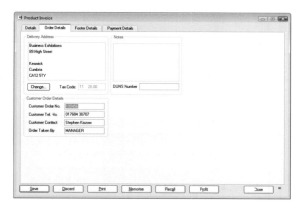

Beware

Any changes made to the delivery details are not saved back to the Customer Record.

Product Invoice Footer Details

Further details, such as Carriage and Settlement Terms, go in the Footer Details:

4 Click on Footer Details tab & enter any Carriage details

5 Record Settlement Terms as appropriate

6 Enter any Global detail if required

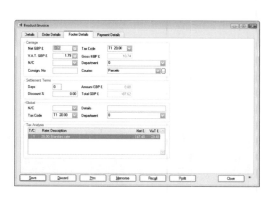

7 Click Save, then Close to finish

Hot tip

For a payment which has already been received and can be allocated against a product invoice, record it using the Payment Details tab.

Don't forget

The Tax Analysis is now shown in the Footer Details section. In earlier versions it was on the Details screen.

Printing an Invoice

Sage 50 gives you the option to print Invoices or Credit Notes either immediately, or at a later date. To print straight away after you have entered all of the details, instead of clicking Save (the Invoice is automatically saved for you) do the following:

92

 From the Product Invoice window click Print

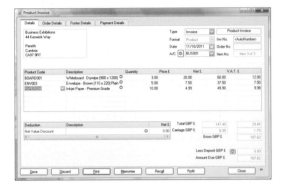

2 Select a suitable file layout

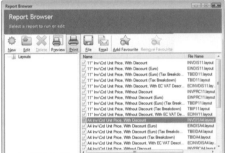

3 Click Print to start generating the report

4 Check that the correct printer is selected in the Print window, choose number of copies to print and click OK

5 If you wish to post the invoice and Update the Ledgers select Preview then click OK, else cancel to print only

6 Click Close to finish

The Service Invoice

To invoice customers for the services you provide instead of products you sell, you should generate a Service Invoice, still using the New/Edit button from the Invoicing Toolbar. An unlimited amount of text can be entered to describe the services provided, and each service can be analysed to a different nominal account. Settlement discounts can be applied, as can carriage charges.

As with Product Invoices, a Service Invoice can be saved to print later or printed straight away. When printing, you have the option to update the ledgers at the same time or leave till later.

1 Click New/Edit on the Invoicing toolbar and select Service in the Format field

2 Change date if different & enter Sales Order No.

3 Enter Customer Account Code, Customer details appear

4 Type service Details here & enter Net cost

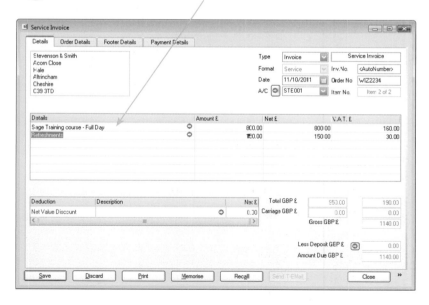

5 Repeat Step 4 as necessary, then click Save

6 Click Close

Hot tip

To avoid having to re-create the same invoice details all the time, you can store a template using the Memorise button or simply select the required item in the invoicing window and click Duplicate.

Don't forget

Sage 50 warns you if a selected customer account has been marked as 'on hold' on the Customer Record.

Hot tip

Select a service item and click on the Edit box or Press F3 to view item details. You can then alter the Posting Details or enter a Job Reference as required.

...cont'd

Service Invoice Order Details

You can record useful additional Order Details on your Service Invoice if required:

Hot tip

If you make a mistake, simply click Discard and start again.

 Click on Order Details tab

2 Enter Delivery Address and any Notes if required

3 Enter Customer Order Details, especially Order No

Hot tip

Any changes made to the delivery details are not saved back to the Customer Record.

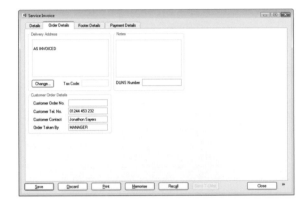

Service Invoice Footer Details

You can record details such as Carriage and Settlement Terms in the Footer Details box:

4 Click on Footer Details tab & enter any Carriage details

5 Record Settlement Terms as appropriate

Hot tip

For payments you have received which can be allocated against the invoice, record the details using the Payment Details tab.

6 Enter any Global detail if required

7 Click Save, then Close to finish

94

The Skeleton Invoice

For information that is regularly repeated when creating an invoice, use the Memorise option to store the invoice as a template. You can then recall this template as and when required, and update it with the new information, thus saving valuable time and reduce keying errors.

This facility is available for both Product and Service Invoices, as well as the Product and Service Credit Notes.

1 On the Details screen enter regularly used details only, such as Customer A/C Ref. & item Details. Omit Price

Hot tip

To bring up a list of all the invoices or orders that you have saved as skeletons or recurring transactions, click the Recurring button from the Invoice toolbar.

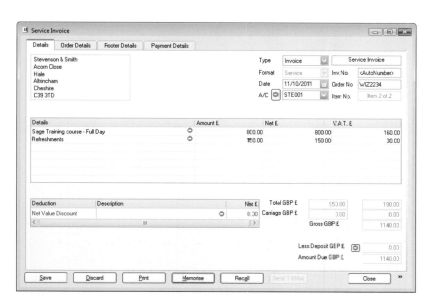

Hot tip

A quick way to alter the date in a Date box is to use the up or down cursor keys to move through the days. Pressing Page Up or Page Down moves through the months.

95

2 Click Memorise

3 Enter Filename and Description then click Save

4 When you need to use a layout, click Recall

Hot tip

To have Sage 50 automatically generate this transaction for you at set regular intervals, just fill in the details in the frequency section of the Memorise window.

5 Select your layout from the list and click Load

Product Credit Note

From time to time goods sent to customers may be returned as faulty, past an expiry date, etc, or the customer may simply have been overcharged by mistake.

Instead of correcting the original invoice, a Product Credit Note can be issued to the Customer, detailing the amount owing to them. When your ledgers are updated, the necessary postings will be made to reflect this amendment. Do the following to create a Product Credit Note:

Hot tip

A VAT only credit note can be raised where a customer has been invoiced and charged tax for goods which are exempt from VAT.

1 Click New/Edit from the Invoicing toolbar and select Credit from the Type field

2 Check Date and enter Order Number if relevant

3 Enter Customer Code, Customer details appear

Beware

In Sage 50 you must always select the Invoice Format, i.e., Product or Service, prior to entering any product or service details. Once you begin to enter these details, the Format box goes to grey and can only be changed by discarding the Invoice and starting all over again.

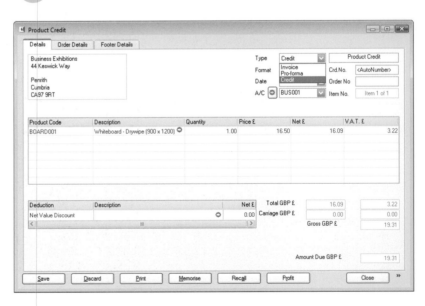

4 Enter the Product Code and the Quantity

5 Repeat Step 4 as required, then click Save to finish

6 Click Close

Process Recurring Transactions

Information that is regularly repeated when creating a Product or Service Invoice or Credit note can be stored and later recalled for use as required or for updating. This feature is particulary useful for any recurring transactions you may have.

If the Frequency details were entered when the recurring transaction skeleton was created and memorised, Sage 50 will remind you automatically on startup if you have any outstanding transactions for processing. You can then choose to immediately post the transactions or process them at a later date as follows:

1 Click Recurring from the Invoicing toolbar to bring up the Memorised Invoices window

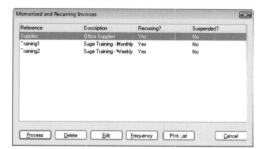

2 Click Process

3 Remove tick here if an entry is not to be processed, then click Process to produce your recurring transactions

4 If any tick was removed in Step 3, click No in next window

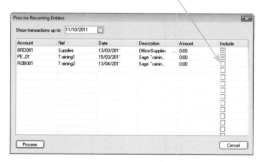

 5 Click OK in the Processing Complete window, then Cancel to close

Hot tip

You can turn off the recurring transaction reminder by selecting the No Recurring Entries at Startup check box in the Bank Defaults window from the Settings menu.

Don't forget

Processing recurring transactions is only available in Sage 50 Accounts Plus and Professional.

Don't forget

When a recurring transaction is processed, only the invoice, purchase order or sales order is produced. You must then remember to post these items manually in order to update the ledgers or allocate any stock.

Updating your Ledgers

After creating your invoices and credit notes, the Update function is used to transfer details to the customer and nominal ledgers and, if appropriate, to amend product records.

Sage 50 gives you the option to print the update report immediately, preview it first so that you can select only certain pages for printing, or to save the report as a file. To perform an Update, do the following:

Hot tip

By regularly updating your stock records, you may find you now have enough free stock to complete outstanding sales orders.

1 From the Invoicing window select invoices/credit notes for updating

2 Click Update to display Output option

3 In the Update Ledgers window click Preview

4 Click OK to generate the update

Beware

Always make sure you select at least one Invoice or Credit Note before using the Update function, otherwise you will be asked if you want to process ALL non-posted invoices and credit notes.

5 On the report, click Print to bring up the Print dialog box, then click OK to print

6 Close to return to the Invoicing window, then Close again

Printing for Batch Invoicing

When you created Invoices or Credit Notes, for both Product or Service, you may have decided to leave printing them until later as a batch. This can often save time when setting up file layouts and having to change the printer stationery.

For example, you may have created four Service invoices which now need printing. You would do the following:

1 From the Invoicing window, select the invoices to print

2 Click Print

3 Select the Layout required

4 Click on Preview button

5 Wait for invoices to generate

6 On the preview, click Print to bring up the Windows Print dialog box, then click OK to print

7 Close to return to the Invoicing window, then Close again

Don't forget

You can reprint your invoices as many times as you wish.

Hot tip

Use the Search button if you wish to print a number of invoices or credit notes that match a particular condition.

Don't forget

Standard layouts can always be edited or new layouts created and saved as necessary.

Producing Reports

The Reports option allows you to produce a wide range of reports about your product and service invoices, as well as your credit notes. Use these reports regularly to keep your business up to date. For example, to print an Invoices Not Posted report:

1 Click Reports from the Invoicing toolbar

2 Click on folder and select report required

3 Click on the Preview button

4 Wait for Report to be generated

Hot tip

Save time: instead of searching through all your invoices for those not yet posted, use the Invoices Not Posted report instead.

Hot tip

Use the Labels button from the Invoicing toolbar to print out your invoice address labels.

5 Check report then click Print

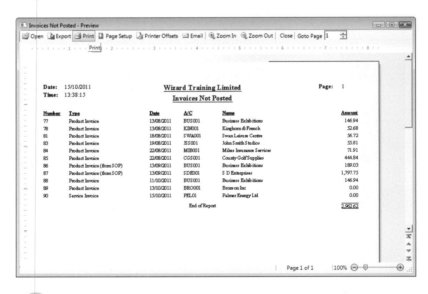

6 Click OK to print report, then Close all windows

8 Processing Sales Orders

Learn how to create Sales Orders and then allocate and despatch stock to these orders as well as how to keep your stock levels up to date.

102 Sales Order Processing Toolbar

103 The Sales Order

105 Allocating Stock

106 Despatching Sales Orders

107 Amending & Printing Sales Orders

108 Sales Orders Reports

Sales Order Processing Toolbar

The SOP toolbar provides a number of features for creating a sales order and then controlling the allocation of stock to that order. Once you are ready to deliver the stock, you can despatch it and Sage 50 will automatically handle the stock record updates. From this toolbar you can also print sales orders, whilst information regarding sales order processing can be easily obtained by using the various report layouts already provided for you.

New/Edit — To Create or View a Sales Order

Allocate — To Allocate Stock to a Sales Order

Despatch — To Despatch a Sales Order

GDN — To Record Delivery of Goods to your Customers

Amend — To Make Changes to a Sales Order

ShortFall — To Run the ShortFall Generator

Recurring — Recall and Process Skeleton or Recurring Transactions

Intrastat — For Intrastat Despatches Confirmation (SOP) window

Print — To Print a Sales Order

Labels — To Print Sales Order Labels

Reports — To Run Sales Order Reports

The Sales Order

Sales orders can be created for the products you supply and sent to customers by using the Enter option from the Sales Order Processing toolbar. Details from your Product records are automatically entered onto the Sales Orders whilst extra details can also be added, such as a delivery address, a customer order number for future reference or a settlement discount.

To create a Sales Order, click Modules, Sales Order Processing from the Sage 50 menu bar, then do the following:

1 Click New/Edit from the Sales Order Processing toolbar

2 Type required date if different and enter Customer Account Code, Customer details appear

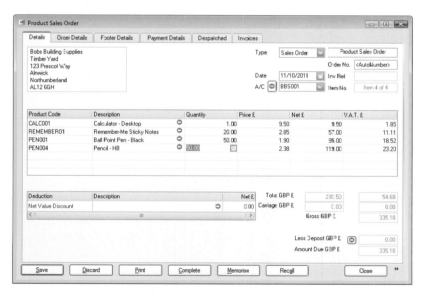

3 Enter the Product Code (use Finder button) and Quantity ordered

4 Repeat Step 3 for any additional products, then when finished click Save

5 Click Close

Hot tip

Use the Message box (i.e., the product code M) to add any text to the main body of the sales order, for example, 'goods supplied free'.

Hot tip

If you use Microsoft Outlook or Google Mail and have set up a default layout you can email your Sales Order by clicking the Email button on the toolbar.

Email

Hot tip

To include special one-off details against a sales item, click the Edit button from the Description box.

...cont'd

Beware

Once a Sales Order has been despatched in part or full, you cannot decrease the quantity of a product to less than the quantity despatched.

Don't forget

Sage 50 will generate an invoice and enter the Invoice Number for you automatically when the order is Despatched.

Hot tip

If you trade physical goods with Member States of the EU, use the Intrastat button for producing trade statistics. The supply of services is excluded. Intrastat replaced customs declarations as the source of trade statistics within the EU and is closely linked with the VAT system. Use the Sage F1 Help key for more information.

Sales Order Details

On the previous page you were shown how to create a Sales Order and save it immediately if no further details need to be entered. Sage 50, however, gives you the option to enter additional details about the order, such as where it should be delivered if different from the main address.

From the Sales Order window, do the following to enter additional order details:

1 Click on the Order Details tab

2 Enter Delivery Address (not yet set up) if required

3 Record any Notes here

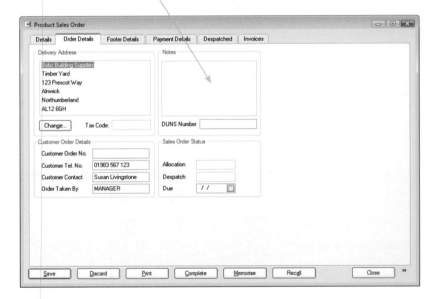

4 Enter any relevant Customer Order Details, such as a Customer Order Number or a Due Despatch date

5 Click Save when finished

6 Click Close

Allocating Stock

Once a Sales Order has been created, stock needs allocating to it before any despatches can be recorded for the Order. Using the Allocate option from the Sales Order Processing toolbar automatically allocates the necessary stock needed for the selected Sales Order.

Sometimes there is insufficient stock available to complete an Order, in which case the Order will be marked as 'Part' complete. There may be times when you have enough stock, but wish to only send part of the Order. In this case you would use the Amend option to make changes to the Order. To allocate batched Sales Orders, do the following from within the Sales Order Processing window:

Hot tip

To view Sales Order details simply double-click on the item.

1 Click on the Sales Orders you wish to Allocate

2 Click Allocate from the toolbar

Don't forget

If Sage 50 cannot allocate all of the necessary stock to the order, a message box is displayed, giving suggestions and possible reasons why not.

105

3 Click Yes to Confirm Allocation of stock

4 Note change in sales order Allocated status, then click Close

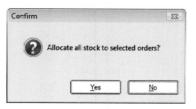

Don't forget

If there is insufficient stock for a Sales Order, the Status 'Part' appears in the Sales Order Processing window. Fully allocated orders display a 'Full' status.

Despatching Sales Orders

Once stock is allocated to your sales orders, it can be despatched at any time. The Despatch option also updates the product records and creates a Product Invoice for the order, as well as printing a Delivery Note.

The product invoices created through Sales Order Processing appears in the Invoicing window. These invoices can be edited, but you cannot change the quantity of the product despatched. They can then be printed and posted to the sales and nominal ledgers in the same manner as invoices created using the Invoicing option.

106

1. From the Sales Order Processing window, select the required Sales Orders

2. Click Despatch from the toolbar

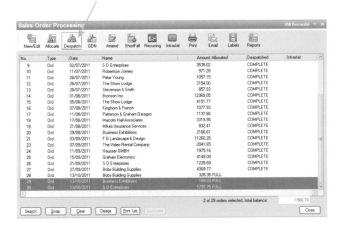

3. Click Yes to print Delivery Notes, create Invoices and Update Stock

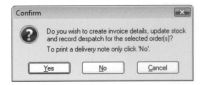

4. Click Print Now for Delivery Notes

5. Select Delivery Note layout, click Generate Report, then Print and Close

Amending & Printing Sales Orders

If you have allocated stock to a sales order, but have not yet despatched all of it, you can amend this allocation. This allows you to despatch a full order by reducing the stock allocation of another customer's order, hence perhaps reducing the number of customers waiting.

To amend the allocation of stock on a sales order

1 Select the Order from the Sales Order Processing window and click Amend

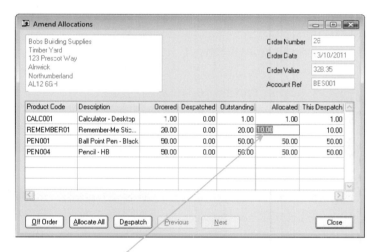

2 Amend the Allocation as necessary

3 Click Close and note change in status from Full to Part

Printing Batched Orders

1 Select orders for printing & click Print

2 Choose layout and click Preview button

3 Click Print, then Close

Don't forget

When you Amend the allocation of stock to a sales order, the allocated status of the order in the Sales Orders window may change to either Full, Part or even no status at all.

Don't forget

Remember that you can raise an invoice even if you have a negative stock situation.

Don't forget

By batching your orders, you can print them all out together after setting up the printer with sales order stationery.

Sales Orders Reports

Sage 50 provides you with a large variety of reports to help you run the Sales Order side of your business. For example, you have the facility to print a picking list for your warehouse from a particular order or the sales order shortage report to show you any shortfalls in the stock.

These reports are generated from the information entered when you created a sales order. To generate, for example, a Sales Order Picking List:

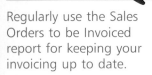

Hot tip

Regularly use the Sales Orders to be Invoiced report for keeping your invoicing up to date.

1 From the Sales Order Processing window, click Reports

2 Click folder and select required Layout

3 Click on Preview to Generate Report

Hot tip

To check how many despatched orders have gone out for a particular time period, use the Despatched Sales Orders report and apply the Order Date Criteria.

4 Enter Criteria i.e. Sales Order number

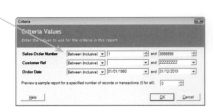

5 Click OK to complete report

6 Click Print, then OK

Hot tip

Use the Labels button from the Sales Order toolbar to quickly print out Sales Order Address or Stock labels.

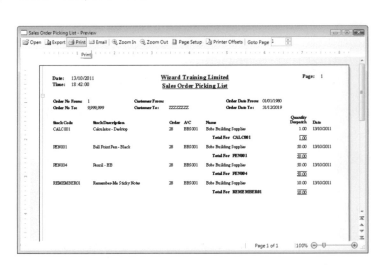

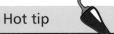
108

9 Purchase Orders

Create and print Purchase

Orders to send to your

suppliers. You will be shown

how to monitor orders

raised and record deliveries

received as well as produce

reports to help track them.

110	**The PO Processing Toolbar**
111	**Creating a Purchase Order**
113	**Placing Orders 'on order'**
114	**Recording Deliveries**
115	**Processing Purchases Manually**
116	**Recording Deliveries Manually**
117	**Printing Batched Orders**
118	**Purchase Order Reports**

The PO Processing Toolbar

From the POP toolbar you can create and print Purchase Orders as well as make amendments to orders you have already created. You have facilities for recording deliveries and producing useful reports about your Purchase Orders, such as a report indicating orders that have been delivered in part or full, or orders that are still outstanding.

New/Edit   To Create or View a Purchase Order

Order   To Put a Purchase Order 'on order'

Deliver   To Record Purchase Order Deliveries

GRN   To Complete a Goods Received Note

Amend   To Make Changes to a Purchase Order

Update   To Automatically Update the Purchase Ledger

Recurring   Recall and Process Skeleton or Recurring Transactions

Intrastat   For Intrastat Arrivals Confirmation (POP) window

Print   To Print a Purchase Order

Labels   To Print Purchase Order Labels

Reports   To Run Purchase Order Reports

Creating a Purchase Order

To record order details of any products you buy from a supplier, use the Enter option from the Purchase Order toolbar. Details entered straight onto the Purchase Order screen are taken directly from the product records for you by Sage 50.

You can also include additional details, such as delivery address or any settlement discount given to you by your supplier, to the order. To create a Purchase Order click POP from the Sage 50 toolbar then follow these steps:

1 Click New/Edit from the POP toolbar

2 Check date and enter Supplier Account Code

3 Supplier details appear here

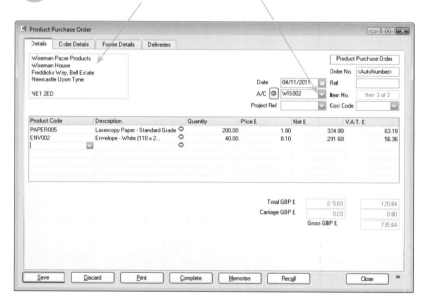

4 Enter the Product Code (use Finder button) & Quantity

5 Repeat Step 4 for additional products and click Save when finished

6 Click Close

Don't forget

If a re-order quantity has been set up on the Product Record, this value is entered automatically for you in the Quantity field.

Don't forget

You can increase but not decrease the quantity for any Purchase Order you have already despatched, whether in full or part.

Hot tip

For non-payment products use the product code M.

...cont'd

Entering Purchase Order Details

You may need to record further details on your Purchase Order, such as delivery details, carriage costs, settlement terms, supplier contact or the name of the person who took your order.

Sage 50 lets you do this through the Order Details or Footer Details tabs. From the Purchase Order window, do the following to enter additional order details:

Hot tip

To edit an existing purchase order simply double-click on it in the Purchase Order Processing window.

1 Click on the Order Details tab

2 Enter Delivery Address if required

3 Record any Notes you wish to add here

112

Hot tip

Save your Purchase Order as a Skeleton if you use these details regularly.

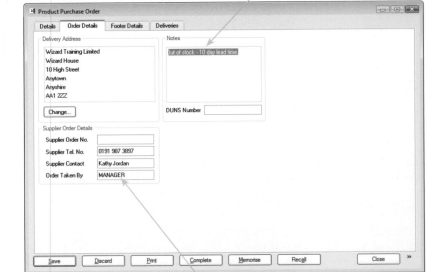

Hot tip

Use the Footer Details tab to record any Carriage or Settlement terms and click the Deliveries tab to view delivery information.

4 You can change who took the order here

5 Enter any relevant Supplier Order Details, such as an Order or Telephone Number

6 Click Save when all details have been entered

7 Click Close

Placing Orders 'on order'

Once a Purchase Order has been created, it has to be placed 'on order' before any deliveries can be recorded for it. The Sage 50 program then updates each product record with the new order details accordingly.

Use the Order option to automatically place a single or batch of Purchase Orders 'on order', as follows:

1 From the Purchase Order Processing window, highlight all orders you wish to place 'on order' by clicking on them

2 Click on the Order button from the POP toolbar

113

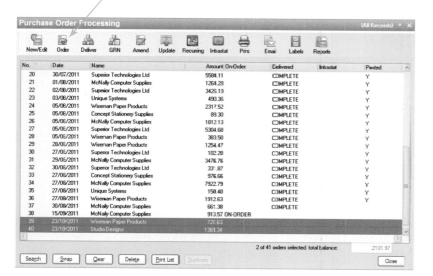

3 Click No to print a copy of the Purchase Order later, else Yes to print now

4 Click Yes to place the selected items 'on order'

5 Note that items are now ON-ORDER, then click Close

Recording Deliveries

To automatically record the complete delivery of stock for Purchase Orders use the Deliver option from the Purchase Order Processing toolbar.

You should remember that Sage 50 always assumes that you have taken full delivery of all the products needed to complete the selected Purchase Order. If a part delivery needs recording, you must do so using the Amend function (see page 116).

To record Purchase Order deliveries do the following:

Beware

When you use the Delivery option it is assumed that you have taken full delivery of all items on the Purchase Order. Note that the Delivery record cannot be altered later.

 1 From the Purchase Order Processing window select any orders you wish to mark as Delivered

2 Click on Deliver from the POP toolbar

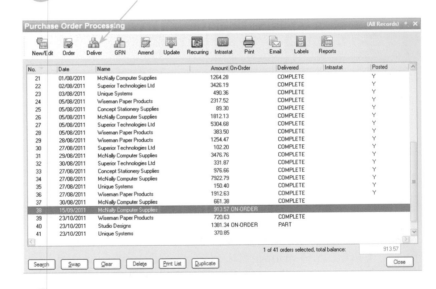

Don't forget

You can only record deliveries for orders which you have already put 'on order'.

 3 Click Yes to Confirm delivery and update stock records, then choose whether to print a GRN now or later

Don't forget

Sage 50 automatically makes adjustments for each product that you mark as delivered.

4 Note the Purchase Order now displays as COMPLETE, then if finished click Close

114

Processing Purchases Manually

To check and keep track of your Purchase Orders use the Amend option. In this window you can manually place them 'on order' (thus updating On Order levels for the appropriate product records), record full or part deliveries of stock against each order and cancel orders.

Placing a Purchase Order 'on order' manually

You have already learned how to place Purchase Orders 'on order' using the Order button (Page 113). However, Sage 50 also allows you to do this manually as follows:

1 From Purchase Order Processing window, select the purchase order you require

2 Click Amend to bring up the Amend Deliveries window

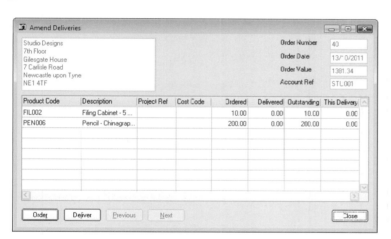

3 Click on the Order button to place 'on order'

4 Note the order now looks normal and the full order quantity appears in This Delivery

5 Click Close

Hot tip

You can cancel a Purchase Order which is 'on order' using the Amend option. Just click Off Order to mark it as cancelled, click Order to put it back 'on order'.

Hot tip

If you use Microsoft Outlook or Google Mail and have set up a default layout you can email your Purchase Order by clicking on Email on the toolbar.

Email

Don't forget

You can use the GRN button from the toolbar to quickly generate a Goods Received Note. Remember, though, that if you set up your GRN Options in Invoice and Order Defaults to 'Do not Generate', Sage 50 will not produce a goods received note and no GRN option will appear on the POP toolbar.

Recording Deliveries Manually

You use the Deliver button from the Purchase Order Processing toolbar only when you have received full delivery of an order.

If you wish to record part deliveries, then you must use the Amend option, though you can still record full deliveries this way as well, should you need to. To record a Purchase Order part delivery, follow these steps:

1 From the Purchase Order Processing window select the order you wish to record a delivery for

2 Click on Amend from the POP toolbar

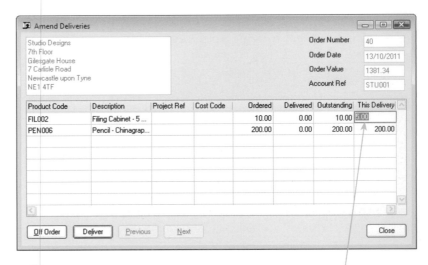

3 Enter part quantity received in the This Delivery column

4 Click on the Deliver button to update your product record details

5 Click Yes to confirm updating of order

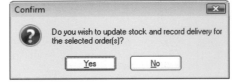

6 Click Close to finish & note status is now PART delivered

Printing Batched Orders

Rather than print your Purchase Orders straight away you may have chosen to save them until later. This is useful if you only have one printer and need to change the stationery. When you are ready you can then print the orders out in batches.

As with all the printing facilities in Sage 50, you can send the Purchase Order direct to the printer, save it as a file or first preview it on the screen. To preview an order and then print it do the following:

1 From the Purchase Order Processing window, select the order for printing

2 Click on Print from the POP toolbar

3 Select required Purchase Order layout

4 Click Preview button

5 On the preview, click Print then click OK

6 Click Close

Hot tip

Save time by emailing your Purchase Orders directly to your Suppliers.

Hot tip

To print a specific selection of Purchase Orders use the Search button facility.

117

Don't forget

If your business trades physical goods with Member States of the EU, use the Intrastat button for producing trade statistics.

Purchase Order Reports

Standard reports have already been set up for you to display any outstanding Purchase Orders, or orders which have already been delivered or part delivered. These reports can be previewed on screen, sent to your printer or saved to a file for previewing or printing later.

To generate a report of any Purchase Orders not yet delivered, do the following:

1 From the Purchase Order Processing toolbar, click Reports

2 Select required layout and click on the Preview button

3 Wait while report starts generating

4 Enter Criteria, if any applies

5 Click OK to generate report

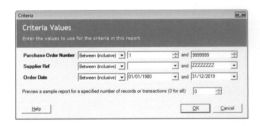

6 Click Print to send to printer, then OK & Close

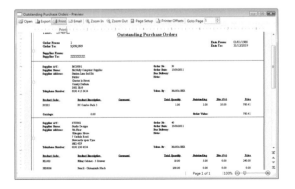

10 Financials

Generate financial reports so you can analyse your business transactions. This includes the Trial Balance, Profit & Loss, the Balance Sheet, the Budget and Prior Year reports plus how to produce a VAT Return and make a submission online.

120   The Financials Toolbar

121   The Audit Trail

123   The Trial Balance

124   Profit and Loss Report

125   The Balance Sheet

126   Quick Ratio Report

127   The Budget Report

128   The VAT Return

131   e-VAT Submissions

132   Financial Reports

The Financials Toolbar

From this toolbar you can generate all the financial reports you need to not only keep track of how your business is doing financially but also trace back and find out when certain transactions took place. The Audit Trail is particularly useful as it is a complete record of your transaction activities, whilst the VAT function gives you all the features you need to produce accurate VAT Returns.

 Audit   To Produce the Audit Trail

 Trial   Run the Trial Balance Report

 P and L   To Produce the Profit and Loss Report

 Balance   To Produce the Balance Sheet Report

 Ratio   Run the Quick Ratio Report

 Variance   To Produce the Budget Report

 Prior Yr   Run the Prior Year Report

 VAT   To Produce a VAT Return

 Verify   To Check for possible Audit or VAT Anomalies

 Reports   To Run Financial Reports

The Audit Trail

The Audit Trail records details about transactions entered into the system and it is a very useful source of information for checking and cross referencing. It may also be referred to when auditing your accounts.

Sage 50 gives you a range of Audit Trail formats providing brief, summary or fully detailed reports which can be previewed, printed directly or saved as a file for use later. A report of deleted transactions can also be printed. Use the Audit Trail regularly to ensure your transactions are being recorded accurately.

To view the Audit Trail:

1 From the Sage 50 menu bar, click Modules then Financials to bring up the Financials window displaying the Audit Trail

Don't forget

Deleted transactions always appear in red.

Hot tip

Transaction codes used in the Audit Trail are explained on Page 49.

Financials												
Audit	Trial	P and L	Balance	Ratio	Variance	Prior Yr	VAT	Verify	Reports			

No	Type	Account	Nominal	Dept	Details	Date	Ref	Ex.Ref	Net	Ta
1203	BP	1200	7100	000	Rent Direct Debit	02/03/2011	DD/STO		1200.00	0.0
1204	BP	1200	2310	000	Hire Purchase Payment	28/03/2011	DD/STO		150.00	0.0
1205	BP	1200	7903	000	Hire Purchase Interest	28/03/2011	DD/STO		5.55	0.0
1206	BP	1200	7100	000	Rent Direct Debit	30/03/2011	DD/STO		1200.00	0.0
1207	BP	1200	7100	000	Rent Direct Debit	27/04/2011	DD/STO		1200.00	0.0
1208	BP	1200	2310	000	Hire Purchase Payment	28/04/2011	DD/STO		150.00	0.0
1209	BP	1200	7903	000	Hire Purchase Interest	28/04/2011	DD/STO		5.55	0.0
1210	BP	1200	7200	000	Electricity Direct Debit	01/05/2011	DD/STO		150.00	12.0
1211	BP	1200	7100	000	Rent Direct Debit	25/05/2011	DD/STO		1200.00	0.0
1212	BP	1200	2310	000	Hire Purchase Payment	28/05/2011	DD/STO		150.00	0.0
1213	BP	1200	7903	000	Hire Purchase Interest	28/05/2011	DD/STO		5.55	0.0
1214	BP	1200	7100	000	Rent Direct Debit	22/06/2011	DD/STO		1200.00	0.0
1215	BP	1200	2310	000	Hire Purchase Payment	28/06/2011	DD/STO		150.00	0.0
1216	BP	1200	7903	000	Hire Purchase Interest	28/06/2011	DD/STO		5.55	0.0
1217	BP	1200	7100	000	Rent Direct Debit	20/07/2011	DD/STO		1200.00	0.0
1218	BP	1200	2310	000	Hire Purchase Payment	28/07/2011	DD/STO		150.00	0.0
1219	BP	1200	7903	000	Hire Purchase Interest	28/07/2011	DD/STO		5.55	0.0
1220	BP	1200	2310	000	Hire Purchase Payment	28/08/2011	DD/STO		150.00	0.0
1221	BP	1200	7903	000	Hire Purchase Interest	28/08/2011	DD/STO		5.55	0.0
1222	SI	BUS001	4000	001	Whiteboard - Drywipe (1000 x 1500)	05/09/2011	74		3861.00	579.1
1223	SI	BRI001	4000	001	Calculator - Pocket	05/09/2011	75		294.00	44.1
1224	SI	PAT001	4000	001	JPC3C Jet Printer	05/09/2011	76		902.50	135.3

Search   Find   Close

2 Use both horizontal and vertical arrow buttons and scroll bars to examine all transaction details

3 When you have finished examining the Audit Trail, click Close

Don't forget

When you clear transactions from the Audit Trail, Sage 50 brings them forward as opening balances in your financial reports.

...cont'd

To print the Audit Trail report

122

Don't forget

The Criteria box options vary according to the type of Audit Trail report you have selected.

Hot tip

You can choose to exclude deleted transactions from your reports and instead, print them as a separate report later.

Hot tip

Make sure you print your Audit Trail reports at least every month to use for reference purposes.

1 From the Financials toolbar click Audit

2 Select Audit Trail Type, e.g. Brief

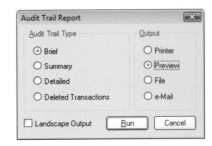

3 Check Output is set to Preview and click Run to continue

4 Enter required Criteria

5 Click here to Exclude Deleted Transactions from the report

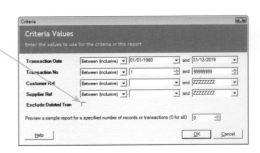

6 Click OK to produce the report

7 If you want to print the report, click Print & OK, then close all windows

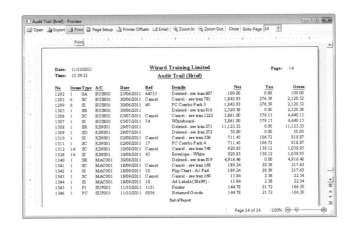

The Trial Balance

This report displays a simple listing of the current balances in all your nominal ledger accounts. It shows total values for both the debit and credit entries for all the nominal codes containing a balance value.

Since Sage 50 controls the double-entry accounting for you, the debit and credit columns will always balance. To produce the Trial Balance report do the following:

1 From the Financials toolbar click Trial. This brings up the Print Output window

2 Ensure Preview is selected and click Run

3 Select period required here

4 Click OK to generate the Trial Balance

5 If you want to print the report, click Print & OK, then close all windows

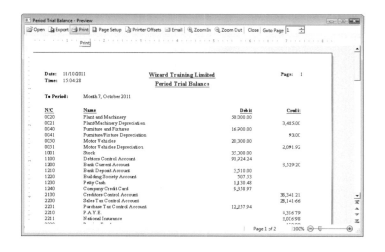

Hot tip

You can run this report for any month as it proves a valuable source of data for management information.

Hot tip

When you open the Financials window, the display automatically jumps down to the bottom of the list so the most recently entered transaction is always highlighted first.

Profit and Loss Report

This important financial report shows whether your business is trading at a profit over a particular period of time. The report can be produced for the current month or a range of consecutive months within your current financial year.

The balances of each of your income and expenditure nominal ledger accounts appear on the standard Profit and Loss report. These categories, i.e. Sales, Purchases, Direct Expenses and Overheads, are grouped together and display a sub-total. The Gross Profit/(Loss) and Net Profit/(Loss) amount is also shown.

Don't forget

Balances are posted before the start of the financial year and so will appear as a prior year adjustment on the balance sheet, not on the Profit and Loss Report sheet.

1. From the Financials window click P and L

2. Ensure Preview is selected and click Run

3. Select period required here

4. Select Default Layout of Accounts (1) then click OK

Beware

Unless you have set up your own layout, ensure you choose the Default Layout of Accounts in Step 4, otherwise you will not generate the correct report.

5. If you want to print the report, click Print & OK, then close all windows

The Balance Sheet

The Balance Sheet shows the financial position of a business at a particular time by outlining its assets (what it owns) and its liabilities (what it owes). There are two main types of assets, fixed and current. Fixed assets are long-term and have material substance such as premises, equipment and vehicles; whilst current assets are continually changing and include stock, debtors, cash accounts, etc.

The Balance Sheet shows the fixed and current assets, as well as the liabilities. By adding together the assets and subtracting the liabilities, the Balance Sheet shows the Capital, or net assets.

1 Click Balance from the Financials toolbar

2 Select Preview & click Run

3 Select period required here

4 Select Default Layout of Accounts (1) then click OK

5 Click Print & OK, then close all windows

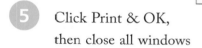

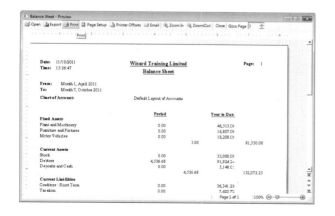

Quick Ratio Report

Using the data available within the system, the Quick Ratio Report allows you to see the current liquidity position of the business. This type of information is necessary for making financial decisions about future investments or developments and will be required by a number of different parties, for example: management, bank managers, shareholders.

These Ratio Reports highlight both the strengths and the weaknesses in the financial position of your business. Credit and debit balances are compared to show the net balance using previously set up nominal account codes. You can edit the report to include other nominal accounts you wish to compare.

To view or edit the quick ratio report

1 From the Financials window, click Ratio

2 To edit the nominal accounts, use Finder button to select Nominal Code required

N/C Ref	N/C Name	Debit	Credit
1100	Debtors Control Account	91924.24	0.00
1103	Prepayments	0.00	0.00
1200	Bank Current Account	0.00	8529.20
1210	Bank Deposit Account	3510.00	0.00
1220	Building Society Account	507.53	0.00
1230	Petty Cash	1130.48	0.00
1240	Company Credit Card	9358.97	0.00
2100	Creditors Control Account	0.00	36341.21
2109	Accruals	0.00	0.00
2200	Sales Tax Control Acco...	0.00	23141.66
2201	Purchase Tax Control A...	12257.94	0.00
3200	Profit and Loss Account	0.00	0.00
4000	Sales North	0.00	180619.53

129737.43

3 Click Print, then Run in Print Output window

4 Select Period

5 Click OK

The Budget Report

The Budget Report displays the current values in your purchases, sales, direct expenses and overhead account codes for the months you select and the year-to-date. Use this report to see how your business actually traded compared with the monthly budget you set against the nominal ledger accounts for the chosen months and the year-to-date.

1 Click Variance from the Financials toolbar

2 Ensure Preview is selected & click Run

3 In the Criteria box enter the From and To Period required

4 Select Default Layout of Accounts (1)

5 Click OK to generate the report

6 Click Print and OK, then close all windows

Hot tip

You can amend your nominal account Budget values at any time by using the Global Changes feature from the Tools menu.

Hot tip

When you run a year end, Sage 50 offers you the option to move the actual monthly values for the year just ended to the budgets for the coming year. This sets the budget values to be what really happened in each month of the year just ended. You can also add a percentage increase to your budget values to reflect any anticipated rise in sales, purchases, costs, etc. for the coming year.

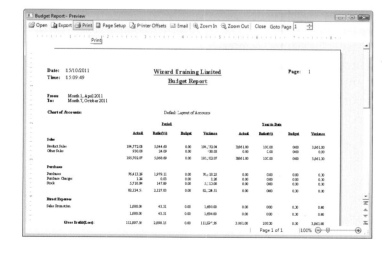

The VAT Return

For businesses that need to submit VAT Return forms to HM Revenue and Customs, Sage 50 provides all the features to enable you to do this quickly and accurately, calculating both input and output tax for you from the information you have entered over the period. This is a prime reason for keeping accurate accounts.

Input tax is the VAT you are charged on your business purchases and expenses. Output tax is the VAT your business charges on its taxable supplies or services. Since Value Added Tax is a tax charged to the final consumer, a business needs to calculate what input tax can be reclaimed and how much output tax needs paying to Revenue and Customs. This is the purpose of the document called the VAT Return.

You have the facility to set up 100 tax codes, but on installation Sage 50 sets the standard UK and EC VAT rates for you, so you will probably not have to change anything. The default is set to the standard rate T1, presently at 20.0%, whilst others you may need are T0 (zero-rated) and T9 (transactions not involving VAT).

Within the nominal ledger there are three accounts, namely Sales Tax Control account (2200), Purchase Tax Control account (2201) and VAT liability account (2202). An accumulated total appears in the Sales account for the output tax charged to your customers whilst another accumulated total appears in the Purchase account for the input tax charged to your business.

When your VAT Return is due, enter the correct date range into the system and the program will calculate the difference between the input and output tax and will inform you of the net VAT due to either the Revenue and Customs or to yourselves.

After reconciling your VAT Return, VAT on the Sales and Purchases Control accounts for this VAT period need to be transferred to the VAT Liability nominal account. When a bank payment to the Revenue and Customs is made or received, the VAT Liability account is cleared, leaving a zero balance.

If you have Internet access, Sage 50 lets you make your VAT submission and payment online as detailed on Page 131, though you will first need to set up a Government Gateway Account. Sage Help on e-VAT shows you how to do this and has a link direct to the HMRC website.

Hot tip

Use the Wizard button to guide you through the various stages of the VAT Return process.

Don't forget

Before reconciling your VAT transactions, you should always back up your data files. Reconciling your transactions sets a flag against each transaction so it is automatically excluded from subsequent VAT Returns.

Hot tip

The Audit Trail VAT column shows whether a transaction is reconciled or not:

• R = reconciled

• N = unreconciled

• a hyphen (-) or a dash (–) = a non-VAT transaction

To produce your VAT Return

1 From the Financials window click VAT to bring up the VAT Return window displaying zero totals

2 Enter the inclusive VAT period dates

3 Click Calculate to calculate totals for this return. You will be informed if any unreconciled transactions are found

Don't forget

Ensure all transactions have been fully reconciled and the Audit Trail checked before running your VAT Return.

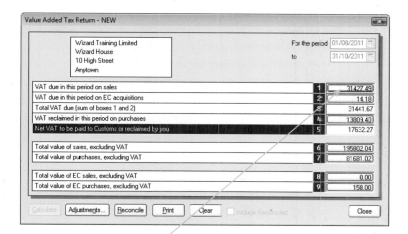

Hot tip

Use the Verify button to quickly run a series of basic checks to highlight possible Audit or VAT anomalies before running the VAT Return.

129

4 Click on a VAT total for a breakdown

5 Double-click on a Tax Code for a transaction breakdown

6 Close each window to return to VAT Return

7 Click Print, Run and OK

8 Click Reconcile & confirm

Hot tip

Three reports are available for printing: Detailed, Summary and the VAT Return. The Detailed and Summary reports give a breakdown of all the totals in each box on the VAT Return.

The VAT Transfer Wizard

Use the VAT Transfer Wizard to guide you through the transfer of your VAT liability once you have successfully reconciled and printed your VAT return.

Hot tip

Use the VAT Transfer Wizard to transfer money from the Sales and Purchase Tax Control accounts to the VAT Liability account.

1 From the Sage 50 menu, click Modules, select Wizards, then click VAT Transfer Wizard

2 Click Yes to confirm you wish to continue

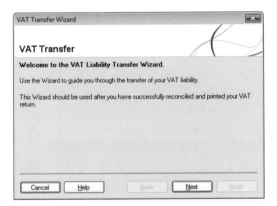

Don't forget

Note that Sage 50 already has the following tax rates set up:

T0 = zero rated transactions

T1 = standard rate

T2 = exempt transactions

T4 = sales to customers in EC

T7 = zero rated purchases from suppliers in EC

T8 = standard rated purchases from suppliers in EC

T9 = transactions not involving VAT

3 Click Next to proceed with the Wizard

4 Work through each screen entering details where required and clicking Next until Confirm Posting Details window

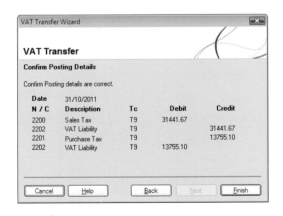

5 Click Finish to confirm details or Cancel to discard

e-VAT Submissions

From April 2010 all large and medium sized companies, most small traders and all newly registered VAT traders, have been required to file their VAT returns online and pay electronically, paper submissions no longer being accepted.

If you didn't choose to enable e-VAT Submission during the setting of your VAT Preferences, you can do so later as follows:

1   Visit the HMRC website and obtain a Government Gateway Account

2   From Settings on the Sage 50 menu bar click Company Preferences

3   Click here to enable e-VAT Submissions

4   Enter your Credentials and Contact Details

5   Click OK to finish

Don't forget

The Submit Return and HMRC Receipts buttons are only visible if you have Enabled e-Submissions in the Company Preferences VAT tab.

Don't forget

You can only make an online VAT submission for a return whose status is Pending or Partial. For a payment, the status must be Submitted but Not Paid.

131

Making an online VAT submission

1   From the Tasks List click Manage VAT

2   Choose the VAT Return required, click Submit Return and follow instructions

3   To pay online click Payment and follow the instructions

Don't forget

To make VAT payments online make sure you have enabled e-Banking in the Bank defaults.

Financial Reports

Sage 50 offers a wide range of Financial Reports that provide management information to enable effective decision-making, planning and forecasting.

A considerable number of reports are set up at installation time, but many can be customised if required for your business by changing the appearance of the layout, the font type or by adding/removing certain text. Refer to Chapter 12 for more details. To generate a report do the following:

1   From the Financials toolbar click Reports

2   Click on folder and select the report layout required

3   Click on the Preview button

4   Wait as report is generated

5   Enter Criteria and click OK to complete the report, then Print

Don't forget

With Sage 50 you can calculate profit and loss for the current month or for any range of consecutive months within your current financial year.

Don't forget

The grouping and positioning of nominal codes on the Financial Reports are determined by the relevant Chart of Account in use.

Don't forget

Information used for creating Financial Reports is taken from the actuals column in the Nominal Ledger Record.

To Verify System

1   Click Verify from Financials toolbar

2   Click OK to run checks

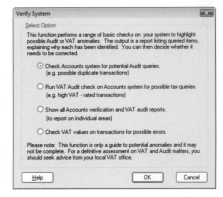

11 Fixed Assets

Learn all about Fixed Asset

Records and how to view

the value of all your assets.

134   **The Fixed Assets Toolbar**

135   **Recording your Fixed Assets**

137   **Fixed Asset Depreciation**

138   **Depreciation and Valuation**

The Fixed Assets Toolbar

This toolbar features options for creating Fixed Asset Records and setting up the method of depreciation, performing valuation of Fixed Assets and the generation of your Fixed Asset reports.

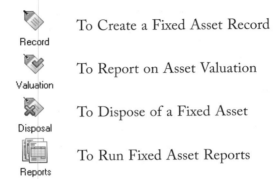

Record — To Create a Fixed Asset Record

Valuation — To Report on Asset Valuation

Disposal — To Dispose of a Fixed Asset

Reports — To Run Fixed Asset Reports

Note:

In recent versions of Sage Accounts programs there is no Fixed Assets button on the navigation bar. Instead, do the following to bring up the Fixed Assets window:

1 On the Sage 50 menu bar, click Modules

2 Click on Fixed Assets Register to bring up the Fixed Assets window

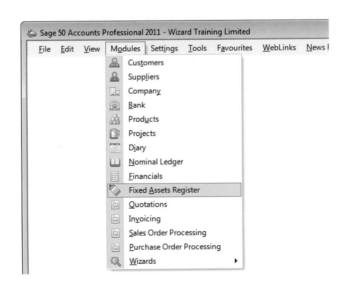

Recording your Fixed Assets

Fixed Assets are items such as office equipment, buildings, machinery, etc. owned by the business. Their depreciation is an expense and can be offset against profits.

However, before recording Fixed Asset information, it is important that the correct method and rate of depreciation be decided upon and applied consistently. Different classes of Fixed Assets are often depreciated at different rates, for example, office furniture may be depreciated at a different rate to motor vehicles.

Sage 50 offers the choice of three depreciation methods: Straight Line, Reducing Balance and Write Off. For the Straight Line method, the asset is depreciated by a fixed percentage (calculated from the original Cost Price of the asset) every month until the asset is reduced to zero. For the Reducing Balance method, the asset is depreciated again monthly by a fixed percentage, but this time the percentage is applied to the new book value of the asset.

The last method, Write Off depreciation, makes one last posting to depreciate the remaining value of the asset.

When ready to enter your fixed assets for the first time you will notice that the Fixed Assets window is empty. As soon as Fixed Asset Records are entered, they will be displayed one record per line. To bring up the Fixed Assets window and view details:

1 From Modules, click Fixed Assets Register

2 Double-click on a record to view details

3 Click Close when done

Hot tip

Have the following information ready before entering your Fixed Asset Records; purchase date of asset and cost price, depreciation method and rate, depreciation balance sheet and depreciation profit & loss nominal codes.

135

Hot tip

To delete an Asset, just highlight it in the Fixed Assets window, then click the Delete button.

...cont'd

Adding Fixed Asset Records

The first time you use the Assets option, the Fixed Assets window will be empty. To add a Fixed Asset record, have all the necessary information to hand, then do the following:

Don't forget

You cannot save a new Fixed Asset record unless the nominal ledger posting details have all been entered.

1 From the Fixed Assets toolbar click Record

2 Enter a unique code to identify asset, no spaces allowed

3 Type a Description & a Serial Number, plus Location if relevant to this asset

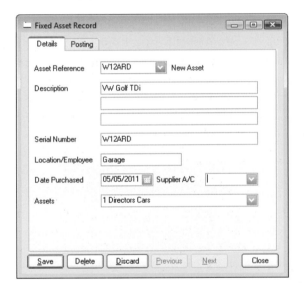

Hot tip

Use the Tab key to move from one data entry box to the next.

4 Enter the Date Purchased

5 If the asset was bought from one of your current Suppliers, select Supplier A/C

6 For reporting purposes select Assets category from the list

Although you have now entered all the relevant details for this asset, before you can save this new record you still need to enter the appropriate nominal ledger posting details. This is explained on the next two pages.

Fixed Asset Depreciation

The Posting Tab in Fixed Asset Record window is used for entering the necessary nominal ledger posting details. Then, when you run the Month End/Year End depreciation posting routines, asset depreciation will be added to the appropriate account code as an expense to your business and will be shown on the Balance Sheet & Profit and Loss Report.

There are four depreciation accounts already set up in the Balance Sheet of the nominal ledger by Sage 50. Every time an asset is depreciated, the amount of depreciation is posted as a credit posting. Codes include 0021 (Plant/Machinery Depreciation), 0031 (Office Equipment Depreciation), 0041 (Furniture/Fixture Depreciation) and 0051 (Motor Vehicles Depreciation).

Similarly, four depreciation accounts are already set up for you in the Profit and Loss section of the nominal ledger. Every time an asset is depreciated, the value of that depreciation is added to the account code as an expense to the company (debit posting). Codes include 8001 (Plant/Machinery Depreciation), 8002 (Furniture/Fitting Depreciation), 8003 (Vehicle Depreciation) and 8004 (Office Equipment Depreciation).

You need to enter the annual rate of depreciation. For the Straight Line method, the value entered will be divided by twelve to calculate the monthly depreciation. For example, to depreciate an asset completely over five years using the straight line method, the Depreciation Rate would be 20%, depreciating at 1.666% monthly until after five years the book value is zero. So, for an item costing £15,000, a depreciation value of £250 would be posted for a term of 60 months.

Where Book Value details are required, then enter the current book value. If the asset is brand new, this should be the same as the Cost Price. If an asset has already been depreciated, then enter the cost price minus depreciation. If the reducing balance method was selected, the Book Value will be used to calculate the depreciation amount. Sage 50 will then automatically reduce this value by the depreciation amount when the month end procedure is run.

Don't forget

The Fixed Asset option does not post depreciation for you, it only records the asset and current value. Use the Month End option to automatically make any depreciation postings.

Beware

Once you have saved a record, the depreciation method can only ever be changed to Write Off.

Hot tip

To record a Fixed Asset Disposal simply click on the Disposal button on the Fixed Assets toolbar and follow the step-by-step Wizard.

Depreciation and Valuation

Setting up a Fixed Asset depreciation posting

Hot tip

From the Fixed Assets window, click the Valuation button to quickly check the totals for cost, current book value and the amount of depreciation that has taken place so far on all of your asset records.

1. From the Fixed Asset Record select the Posting tab

2. Select Department where appropriate

3. Enter the nominal ledger Balance Sheet account code and the nominal ledger Profit & Loss account code

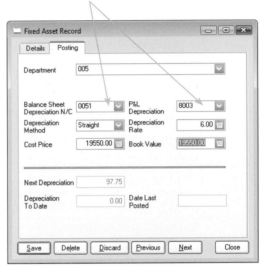

4. Select Depreciation Method & enter annual percentage Rate of Depreciation

5. Enter Cost Price (Net) & the current Book Value then click Save to store the details

Don't forget

Sage 50 lets you save both non-depreciating assets as well as depreciation assets.

Valuation of Fixed Assets

To see details about the current value of your assets including total cost, previous total depreciation and total current book value:

1. From the Fixed Assets window click Valuation to bring up the Asset Valuation window

2. When finished, click Close

138

12 The Report Designer

Layout a report, add filters, calculations and criteria.

140 The Report Designer

141 Creating a New Report

144 Modifying an Existing Report

The Report Designer

When you first install Sage 50, you can immediately generate and print all of the reports and stationery to suit most business needs. If you use stationery supplied by Sage, the data should fit in the pre-printed stationery forms without adjustment.

There will be occasions though when you need a new report not already supplied, or you need to modify an existing one to suit your specific needs. The Report Designer lets you do all of this to meet any specific requirements you may have.

The Report Designer included as an integral part of Sage 50 is actually a complete windows application on its own. The Designer has its own Title Bar, Menu Bar, and Desktop area on which you can open multiple document windows. Each document window can hold an entirely separate layout file, which means you can work on several layouts at once, if you wish. You can also convert old Report Designer layouts from earlier versions to the new format. To run the Report Designer do the following:

1 On the Sage menu bar select Tools, then Report Designer

2 Double-click on a folder for a list of existing layouts

Hot tip

For more details about the Report Designer simply press F1.

Hot tip

Use the Report Designer to quickly create or modify your own reports, stationery layouts, letters and labels.

Creating a New Report

The following example shows you how to create a Customer Balance and Credit List for a single customer or a range of customers using the Report Wizard. The report contains the Customer's account reference, company name and account balance, together with their credit limit. The report is sorted to show the customer with the lowest balance first. The report also displays a balance total.

Don't forget

When the Wizard is finished the Report Designer appears with the new report or layout open ready for you to work on or preview.

1 Click File, New, Report from the Report Designer menu

2 Select Customer option and click Next

3 Double-click on a field table & select variable required from the list

Hot tip

To save time you can double-click the required variable to copy it to the Report Variables view.

4 Click Add (▶) to copy to Report Variables view

5 Repeat selection for all required variables & click Next

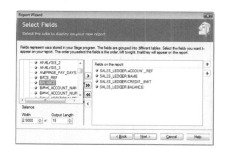

6 Click Next again as grouping not required

Hot tip

For information about the various variables, click the Variable Info button. You can then print out the variable list for later reference.

7 Select SALES_LEDGER.BALANCE for the Sort

8 Click Add, confirm Ascending & click Next

Hot tip

Use the Favourites option to access the most frequently used reports.

...cont'd

9 Select SALES_LEDGER.BALANCE from Totals

10 Click Remove (◄)

11 Click Next

12 Remove all but Customer Ref & Transaction Date from the Selected criteria window

13 Click Next

14 Enter a report name then click Finish to generate the report layout

The Report Designer now generates the appropriate report layout for you. You will be able to see how the layout is divided into sections, i.e. Page Header, Details, Page Footer, etc. Remember though that depending upon your own options and settings, the initial layout may differ to that shown. For example, you may have to manually enable Criteria, add a Page Header or Footer, etc.

If the layout is not as required, you can modify the report later. First you need to check that it provides the information you require by running a report preview.

...cont'd

Previewing your Report

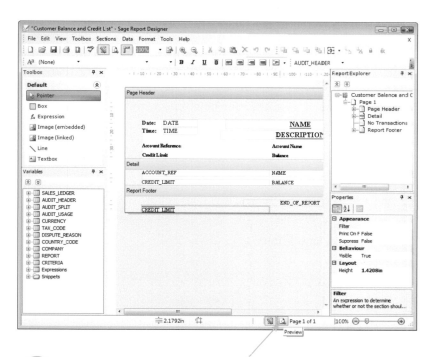

Hot tip

If your new report has no Page Header or Footer, remove the tick from the Use Data Path for Reports option in Company Preferences and try creating the report again.

1 Click Preview to run your new report

2 Enter Criteria details here

3 Click OK to run the report

4 To save, select Save As from File menu, enter a filename and click OK

5 To close, click on File and Exit

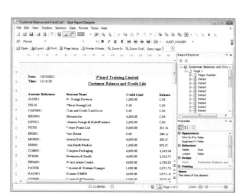

Hot tip

To speed up report design you can cut and paste groups of variables between two reports.

143

Beware

Be careful not to overwrite any existing reports. They may be useful to you later.

Modifying an Existing Report

The Report Designer lets you modify existing report layout files and default reports supplied with the program. These will, however, need saving under a new filename.

As an example, you can modify the report just created and saved to include only those customers having a balance greater than £1000. This is called a filter, which is embedded in the report layout. Assuming you saved your new report under Customers, to make this change it is easier to start from the Customers option:

1 From the Customer toolbar click on the Reports option

2 Open correct folder, select your report and click Edit

3 Click Data, Filters

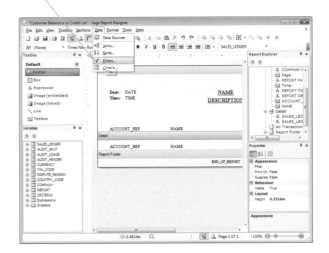

4 Double-click SALES_LEDGER.CREDIT_LIMIT here

5 Type > and 1000 here, then OK

6 Click OK, Preview & Save

Don't forget

To remove your company's name and address from all your layout files, select Company Preferences from the Settings menu on the Sage 50 toolbar. Click on the Reporting tab and deselect the Print Address on Stationery check box, then click OK.

Hot tip

You can edit some Fixed Reports and save them to a new filename. The original report remains unchanged and your new report is added to the list.

Hot tip

If you make a mistake designing the report, select immediately the Edit Undo option from the Edit menu.

13 Opening Balances

This chapter explains how

to enter opening balances

for your customer, supplier,

nominal and bank accounts

as well as your products.

146 Introduction

147 Standard VAT – O/B

148 VAT Cash Accounting – O/B

149 Clearing Opening Balances

151 Entering Balances Mid-Year

152 Nominal Ledger & Bank A/c

154 Product Opening Balances

Hot tip

Print off a copy of the Opening Balances checklist from the F1 Help system to guide you during set up.

Don't forget

Posted Opening Balances for your customers and suppliers are displayed in the Trial Balance Report, which needs clearing before entering any Opening Balances for your nominal ledger accounts, bank accounts and products.

Hot tip

Note that these are the Nominal Codes used in the Trial Balance:

1100 = Debtors Control Account

2100 = Creditors Control Account

9998 = Suspense Account

Introduction

It is important to set up your opening balances correctly and in the right order. All accounts remain at zero until you enter opening balances for your Customers, Suppliers, Nominal, Bank and Products.

Where opening balances are carried forward, accurate figures need to be entered to reflect the true financial position of the business, for example, its Debtors, Creditors, Nominal Ledger Trial Balance, as well as its Stock.

Standard VAT and VAT Cash Accounting

Standard VAT calculates the VAT return on the invoices/credits you have raised for your customers or received from your suppliers, and any bank/cash payments or receipts or journal entries with vatable tax codes.

Customer opening balances can be entered as lump sum balances. It is recommended, however, that each outstanding invoice and credit note should be entered separately for cross referencing. Recording separate transactions will also provide accurate aged debtors analysis.

The second method, the VAT Cash Accounting scheme, is where the VAT return is calculated on the invoices/credits which you have received payment for from your customers or you have paid to your suppliers. It also includes any bank/cash payments or receipts or journal entries with vatable tax codes.

With VAT Cash Accounting each invoice and credit note must be entered for your customers individually, with the correct tax code.

The same Standard VAT and VAT Cash Accounting conditions apply for entering opening balances for suppliers. Again, it is recommended for Standard VAT that separate transactions be recorded for outstanding invoices and credit notes to match up with payments later instead of grouping them all together in one opening balance. Separate transactions will again provide accurate aged creditors information.

Standard VAT – O/B

With the Standard VAT accounting method opening balances can be entered as a lump sum or individual transactions. You set up your customer balances using the Customer Record, accessed by using the Customers button on the Sage 50 toolbar.

Where customer information exists already, you can refer to the Aged Debtors Analysis and Detailed Customer Activity reports for cross referencing purposes and for checking that opening balances are recorded accurately. The Aged Creditors and Detailed Supplier Activity reports are also available for your suppliers.

To enter customer Opening Balance details

1 From the Customers window click on the required record, then click Record on the toolbar

2 Click here to set up the Opening Balance

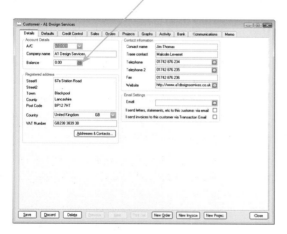

3 Enter invoice/credit note number, the original transaction date or last date of previous financial year, Type and Gross

4 Click Save to record details or Cancel to discard

Hot tip

Simply follow the same procedures as for Customers when entering opening balances for your Suppliers.

Hot tip

An Opening Balance can be entered as one total amount only if a detailed breakdown is not required.

Don't forget

T9 is set as the default non-vatable tax code.

VAT Cash Accounting – O/B

Using this particular scheme each customer invoice and credit note needs entering individually with the correct tax code because VAT is only considered when payment is being made. The opening balances can be entered using the Batch Invoices or Credits screens.

To enter customer Opening Balance details

1 From the Customers window click on the required record, then click Record on the toolbar

2 Click here to set up the Opening Balance

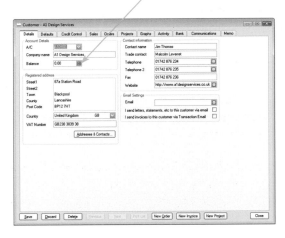

3 Enter invoice/credit note number

4 Enter invoice/credit note number, the original transaction date or last date of previous financial year and Type

5 Enter Net amount. If you want to enter a single opening balance, enter total net amount of all invoices here

6 Tax Code and VAT are entered for you. Check, then click Save

Clearing Opening Balances

When opening balances for your customers and suppliers are saved, they are posted to the Trial Balance. These entries need clearing or they will be duplicated when posting opening balances for your nominal ledger accounts. This will produce an incorrect Balance Sheet.

Before you start, make a note from your Trial Balance of the values of your Debtors and Creditors Control Accounts, your Sales Tax and Purchase Tax Control Accounts and your Suspense Account and whether each one is a debit or a credit, for example:

Trial Balance

Name	TC	Debit	Credit
Debtors Control Account	T9	30,687.19	
Creditors Control Account	T9		21,189.78
Suspense	T9		9,497.41
BALANCE		30,687.19	30,687.19

Once the relevant details have been noted, a Journal Entry from the Nominal Ledger needs to be made to clear the balances. Using the details from the above example, the entry would be as follows:

Journal Entry

Name	TC	Debit	Credit
Debtors Control Account	T9		30,687.19
Creditors Control Account	T9	21,189.78	
Suspense	T9	9,497.41	
BALANCE		30,687.19	30,687.19

Don't forget

Remember to print a copy of your Trial Balance Report BEFORE clearing the opening balances.

Hot tip

When entering journal entries into the transaction table, use opposite values from the Trial Balance, i.e. Debit (+) and Credit (-).

Beware

The journal entry can only be saved when the value in the Balance box is zero.

...cont'd

Once you have noted what entries you need to make, you can add them to the Journal. When you process these entries, the opening balances in the Trial Balance will be cleared. To make the entries do the following:

Always bear in mind that for a journal entry, the VAT is neither calculated nor posted for you to the VAT control account record. You have to do this manually.

1 From the menu bar click Modules, then Nominal Ledger

2 Click on Journals from the Nominal Ledger window

3 The Reference entry is optional. Type a reference if desired then check for correct Date

4 Enter details for both the credit and debits

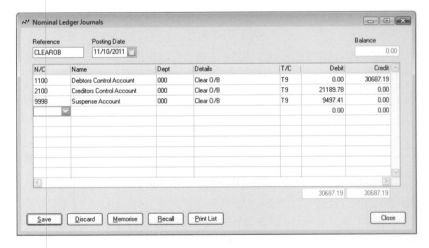

N/C	Name	Dept	Details	T/C	Debit	Credit
1100	Debtors Control Account	000	Clear O/B	T9	0.00	30687.19
2100	Creditors Control Account	000	Clear O/B	T9	21189.78	0.00
9998	Suspense Account	000	Clear O/B	T9	9497.41	0.00
					0.00	0.00
					30687.19	30687.19

Reference: CLEAROB — Posting Date: 11/10/2011 — Balance: 0.00

5 Note, the default Tax code of T9 is entered for you by Sage 50

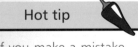

If you make a mistake just click on the Discard button and start again.

6 Check total Debit and Credit are equal and a zero balance is displayed in the Balance box

7 Click Save to process your journal or Discard to cancel

8 Click Close to return to Nominal Ledger window

Entering Balances Mid-Year

Sage 50 needs Opening Balances in order to produce accurate financial statements. Since all accounts in all the ledgers have a zero balance when the program is first installed, it is important that the Opening Balances are entered as soon as possible. Without them your financial statements will not be up to date and accurate.

It is, however, quite possible to start using Sage 50 at any time through your financial year, and then enter the Opening Balances as they become available. For instance, if you have been in business for some time you will already have stock, products, customers and suppliers. You will have a transaction history. When you first start to use Sage 50 you will set up Records for your Customers, Suppliers, Products etc. This is when you can start to enter some Opening Balances.

If you do start to use Sage 50 part way through your financial year, you should contact your accountant as soon as possible for a detailed list showing all your outstanding Debtors and Creditors. You can then use this as the Opening Balances for your Customers and Suppliers.

You also need to ask for a Trial Balance from your accountant, which will give you the Opening Balances for each Nominal Ledger and Bank account.

You must at all times make sure that the information you enter is accurate. If you need to enter Opening Balances part way through your financial year, you will probably have a lot of Nominal Ledger opening balances to enter as well! It is important, therefore, that you enter these accurately otherwise your balance sheet will be incorrect.

You will also need to enter any year-to-date values from your Profit and Loss accounts. Your accountant should be able to provide you with this.

Hot tip

When you start using Sage 50 for the first time and you set up Product records, this is also a good time to have a stock take so that you know the details you are entering are accurate. Sage 50 can only produce accurate reports if the information you enter is correct. This is also a good time to check that Customer and Supplier details are still up to date.

151

Don't forget

If you do not enter a Cost Price in the Opening Product Setup box, then the product code is recorded as zero. This could affect your finance reports later.

Nominal Ledger & Bank A/c

When entering opening balances for your Nominal Ledger or Bank account, double-entry postings are applied by Sage 50. For example, if you post a debit opening balance of £1,000 to your Building Society account (1220 by default), Sage 50 will automatically post £1,000 as a credit to your Suspense Account (9998 by default).

After you have entered all your Nominal Ledger and Bank account opening balances, the balance of the Suspense Account should be zero again. A new Trial Balance needs to be printed to check that opening balances have been included for all your nominal accounts. If you still have a balance in your Suspense Account (i.e. it is not zero), an opening balance may have been omitted or a debit or credit misposted.

Nominal ledger opening balances

1 From the menu bar click Modules, then Nominal Ledger

2 Select the required account & click on the Record button

3 Click the O/B button to enter the balance

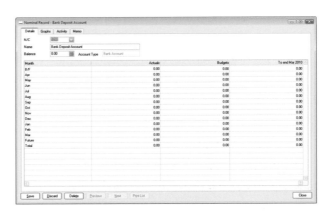

4 Enter opening balance details

5 Click Save then Close

Don't forget

If you have money in the bank or building society, their statement shows you have a balance under the credit column. They owe you that money, you are the creditor. When this money is recorded in your accounts, such asset balances are recorded the opposite way round as debits. If you have money in your bank or building society, the balance must be entered as a debit.

152

Hot tip

Enter an opening balance for each nominal account that appears on your Trial Balance.

Bank Opening Balances

You can also set up a Bank account Opening Balance directly from the Bank Record. To do this follow these steps:

1 From the Sage 50 menu bar click Modules, then Bank

2 Click on the Bank Record you wish to set up an Opening Balance for and click on Record

3 Click the O/B button

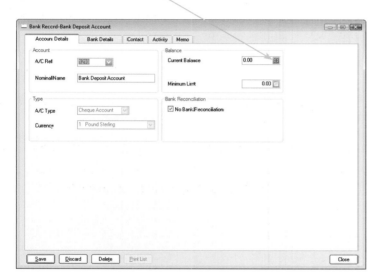

4 Enter Date if different. Then enter the opening balance as a Receipt or Payment. If you have money in your bank, this will be a Receipt

5 Click Save to record the Opening balance information, then close the Bank record

Product Opening Balances

When you create a Product Record, you will probably enter an Opening Balance for that product if you already have some in stock. However, there will be times when you need to enter an Opening Balance at a later date to that when the Record was first set up.

If you do the latter, when you save the Opening Balance for a product, Sage 50 posts an Adjustment In transaction, which appears on the product reports. The valuation report will show the opening stock quantity at the cost price entered. To set up a Product Opening Balance:

Don't forget

If you have selected the Ignore Stock Levels check box, you will not be able to enter an opening balance for this product.

1 From the Sage 50 menu bar click Modules, then Products

2 Select the Product requiring an opening balance

3 Click Record, then click O/B button on the In Stock box

Hot tip

To store a JPEG image of the item with the stock record just select the Web tab then click on the Add button in the Image section.

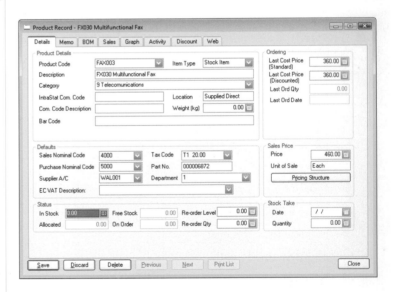

Don't forget

Remember to enter the Cost Price for the Product when you set up the Opening Balance.

4 Enter Opening Balance details here

5 Click Save to return to the Products Record, then Close

14 Data Management

This chapter shows you important routines and procedures you need to use regularly to maintain your data integrity. Backing up of data is the most important as problems could occur at any time.

156 Backing Up Data

157 Restoring Data

158 Changing Global Values

160 Importing Data

162 File Maintenance

165 Write Off, Refund & Return

168 Posting Contra Entries

169 Run Period End Functions

172 Clearing Audit Trail and Stock

Backing Up Data

Regular data backup (at least once daily) is essential in case of system error, when valuable data can be corrupted and sometimes lost. If this happens, you can at least restore important data files, reports and/or layout templates from your most up-to-date backup. A backup routine is provided by Sage 50 that remembers which drive or location you last used, but this can be changed to save to any drive and/or directory you require.

Backing up procedures vary from business to business; some use five disks for Monday to Friday and repeat their usage the following week. The important thing is to backup your data at least once a day! Sage 50 always prompts you to back up when you Exit the program, but to perform a backup at any other time, do the following:

Don't forget

Always keep your backups in a safe and secure place.

1 From the Sage 50 menu, click on File, then Backup

2 Click No, unless you first want to check your data

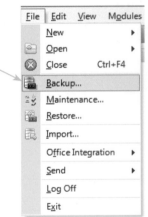

Don't forget

Although you are given the option of checking your data before doing a backup, it is advisable to click No and take the backup first, just in case errors are detected and you need copies of the data. Then take a final backup, this time running the data check procedure, if required.

3 To backup using the default Filename choose a Location and click OK; else to make changes follow Steps 4–5

4 To choose which File Types to backup use Advanced Options tab

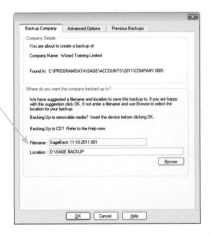

5 Click OK

Restoring Data

Hopefully you should never have to restore your files, but should you be unlucky and suffer data loss or corruption, the Restore procedure allows you to revert to a previous backup. The backup you use to restore data is up to you, but it will normally be the most recent.

The Restore facility allows data from your backup disks to replace your old data by erasing it and starting again. It is, therefore, very important to correctly label disks when you take a backup, and always keep them in a safe place. You may even consider keeping a second copy somewhere other than on the premises in case of fire or theft!

Since the restore procedure erases your old data, any data you entered after the last backup is lost and will need to be entered again, so ensure you take frequent backups. Make sure that the Restore is first necessary, then do the following:

1 From the Sage 50 menu click on File, then Restore

2 Click OK to restore data files from default drive, else go to Step 3

3 If you are restoring from a different drive, enter location here

4 Click OK

5 Click OK to confirm and perform the data restore

Hot tip

It is always advisable to run the Check Data option from File, Maintenance after you have restored your data.

Beware

Restoring data will completely erase your current Sage 50 data and replace it with data from your backup disks.

157

Don't forget

If you cancel whilst performing a Restore, Sage requires you to log in again.

Changing Global Values

There are certain values in Sage 50, such as Credit Limits, that have applications throughout the program. From time to time certain record values may need changing for all your records or for a selected group. To save time, these values can be changed quickly and easily by using the Global Changes Wizard. The Wizard guides you with on-screen instructions to make the necessary changes where required.

Values within the customer, supplier and nominal ledger records can be changed as well as certain values within your product records, for example the product sales price could be increased globally by 5% or the re-order level increased for a range of products. To run the Wizard:

1 From the Sage 50 menu, select Tools

2 Click on Global Changes to start the Wizard, then click Next to continue

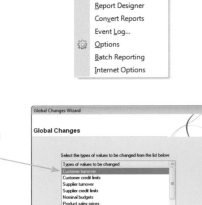

3 Select the area where you want to make a Global Change

4 Click Next to continue

 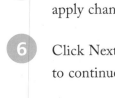
5 Select items to apply change to

6 Click Next to continue

7 Select type of change and enter a value before progressing

8 Click Next to continue

Hot tip

To exit from a wizard at any point, choose the Cancel button or press ALT + F4.

9 Check correct items are to be processed

10 Click Next to continue

11 Check that the details are correct. If you need to make any changes, use the Back button until you get to the appropriate screen, make the changes, then keep clicking Next to get back to this screen

Beware

Also use the Global Changes Wizard to set up product sales and purchase prices, Discount Rates, Re-order Levels and Re-order Quantities for your Products.

159

12 Click Finish to action the changes

Whilst the Global Changes Wizard allows you to make changes quickly and easily, be very careful when using it and always double-check your values because when you click Finish, the changes you have entered are actioned immediately. In some cases these are quite major changes, such as increasing all product sales prices by a stated percentage. If you were to accidentally enter the wrong percentage, you cannot easily undo the resulting changes!

Beware

Always check you have entered the correct information as you may not be able to easily undo changes.

Importing Data

It can be very laborious entering a lot of data into certain records so Sage 50 lets you import data into the following record types – customers, suppliers, products and nominal ledger – provided, of course, it conforms to the correct file format. A group of new records can be created and imported directly into Sage 50 or existing records updated with new details, replacing records being entered individually.

The text can be easily produced using any program which allows you to save the file in text format (.txt), for example, a word processing, spreadsheet or accounts package. The text must be in a specific format otherwise it will not be imported correctly and errors will be reported. These files are called CSV files (Comma Separated Values).

The following rules apply:

- A comma separates each unit of data, i.e. B01,Bolt,100,0.2

- Each data record takes up a single line

- Each data record is terminated by pressing ENTER

- Any spaces at the start or end of a data unit are ignored, but spaces within data units are included

- Use quotes to include commas within a data unit, i.e. "25, Bell Lane"

- Each data unit in a record must be entered in strict order to avoid being imported incorrectly

- Two consecutive commas (,,) forces a move to the next data unit

An example of three typical CSV data records:

1,SI,BROWN,4000,2,Supplies,03/10/08,,27.15,T1,Y

2,SC,WHITE,4000,2,Credit,14/10/08,,35.00,T1,N

3,PI,BLACK,5000,4,Equipment,25/11/08,,52.50,T1,Y

To Import a Data File

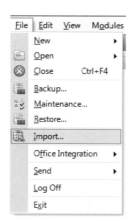

1 From the Sage 50 menu select File, then click Import

2 Click Next then select Import Type here

3 Click Next to continue

4 Select import format and click on Browse button

5 Enter Name of File to Import or select from list

6 Click Open then Next, Next again, then Finish

Don't forget

The inclusion of a SPACE between two commas (,) causes the existing data to be erased.

Don't forget

Importing a blank unit of data does not overwrite existing data – it simply leaves it intact and forces a move to the next data unit. Use this feature for changing only selected data in a record.

Beware

A list of file import details is available from the help facility for customer and supplier records, nominal ledger audit trail transactions, stock records and all stock transactions.

File Maintenance

Sage 50 provides five important options to manage and check the validity of your data files. These features include checking for input errors, allowing manual data error corrections, data compression, re-indexing and building new data files.

Error Checking

You should use the Check Data facility to check the validity of your data files. If necessary you can then make corrections where required. This facility needs to be run regularly, when making backups and after restoring data.

Hot tip

Use the Check Data option on a daily basis to check for errors, so they can be quickly detected and rectified.

Don't forget

If there are problems whilst checking the data, a File Maintenance Problem Report dialog box appears which includes a Summary and details of Comments, Errors or Warnings.

162

1 From the Sage 50 menu select File, then click on Maintenance

2 From the File maintenance window click Check Data

3 Checking Data Files box shows the progress

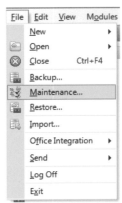

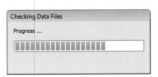

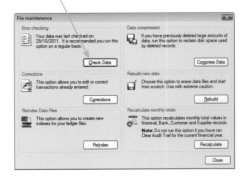

4 Check out the details using Tabs

5 Click Fix to correct errors, else Close

Hot tip

To print out an error report, select the category tab required from the File Maintenance Problems Report dialog box and click the Print button.

Correcting Transactions

Any mistakes made while entering transactions can be corrected using the Corrections option from the File Maintenance window. These transactions, however, can only be edited or deleted if they are still held in the Audit Trail. To correct a transaction:

1 Click Corrections from the File Maintenance window

2 Select transaction to correct

3 Click Edit item

4 For changes to the account, details, reference or date, make your corrections here

5 For more changes click Edit

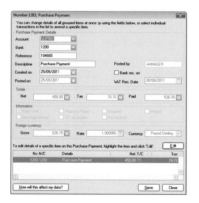

6 To change the details, amounts or VAT code, make your corrections here. Use Edit to change Payment Ref

7 Close and Save

Hot tip

Use the View button to amend any reference for payments/receipts made against a transaction.

Hot tip

Use the Find button to search for transactions.

163

Don't forget

Journal entries cannot be amended using the View button. To do so you must select the Journals option from the Nominal Ledger toolbar and make the adjustment by posting a journal entry with the opposite values.

...cont'd

Deleting Transactions

You can delete a transaction provided it has not already been reconciled on the VAT Return. So you have a record of all changes, a copy of the deleted transaction then appears at the end of the Corrections window list in red. To delete a transaction:

 Select transaction in the Corrections window and click Delete item button

Check this is the correct item and click Delete

Click Yes to confirm

Data Compression

When there has been a lot of activity, such as deletion or amendments of any records, use the Compress Data option to produce a new set of data files. Sage 50 will then reduce file size by removing these deleted records, freeing up disk space. To perform data compression, do this:

Click Compress Data from the File Maintenance Box

Click Compress

Click Close

Rebuild

This Sage 50 option is for creating a new or selected set of data files. From the File Maintenance window:

Click Rebuild

Select files and click OK

Write Off, Refund & Return

Use these options to carry out accounting procedures that affect your customer and supplier accounts, e.g. cheque returns, invoice refunds and outstanding invoice transactions. The way you record these depends on your VAT method.

Refunds

Use this facility for credit notes, payments on account and invoices where a money refund is required rather than a replacement of goods or provision of services. If you are using the Standard VAT Scheme, do the following:

1 From the Suppliers Tasks list select Write Off/Refund

2 Select where you want to make the amendments

3 Click Next

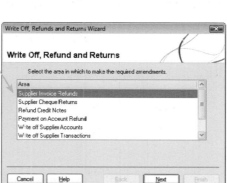

4 Select the account to whom the invoice refund is to be made

5 Click Next to Continue

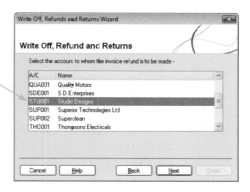

Don't forget

Sage 50 procedures for these functions vary depending on whether you are using the Standard VAT Scheme or VAT Cash Accounting.

Hot tip

For VAT Cash Accounting the transaction needs writing off manually. For more information, refer to Recording Refunds (VAT Cash Accounting) section of the Sage Help.

165

Hot tip

To find out if you are able to reclaim VAT paid on a Write Off, call HM Revenue and Customs.

...cont'd

Beware

Remember that this option is NOT suitable for anyone using VAT Cash Accounting as it does not adjust the VAT value for you.

Hot tip

If the presented summary of information is incorrect, simply use the Back button to return to the appropriate box and modify.

6 Select the invoice being refunded

7 Click Next to continue

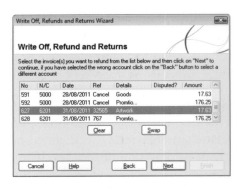

8 Select the bank account you wish to post to

9 Click Next

10 Enter the correct date to use for the transaction

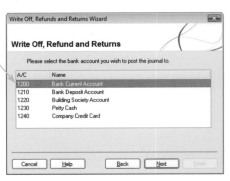

11 Click Next

12 A summary now appears

13 Check carefully that it is all correct. Use the Back button if you need to make any change, else go to Step 14

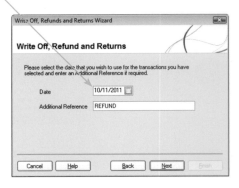

14 Click Finish to post changes to your ledgers

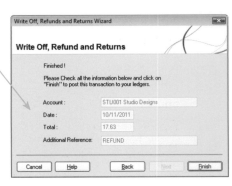

Write Off

At times a customer will not or cannot pay an outstanding debt, so the amount has to be written off to a bad debt account. The steps are very similar to a Refund, but fewer. Just select the appropriate Write Off for Step 2 on Page 165 and follow the simple instructions.

Cheque Returns

Occasionally, you may need to record a cheque from a customer that you wish to cancel or that the bank has returned. If you use the Standard VAT Scheme, do this:

1 From the Customers Tasks list select Write Off/Refund

2 Click Customer Cheque Returns and Next

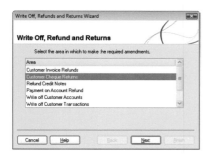

3 Select account, and click Next

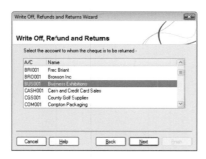

4 Select the cheque and carry out Steps 9–14 on Page 166

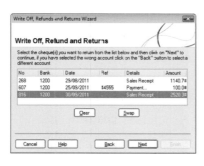

Don't forget

Using a credit note to refund an outstanding customer invoice is known as allocating the credit note to the customer invoice.

Don't forget

When a sales credit note is posted to the customer's account it assumes the same reference as the refunded invoice.

Don't forget

To record a refund using the Write Off, Refunds and Returns Wizard, the refund must need to be fully refunded and must not have been removed from the Audit Trail. If it has been removed or you need to make a partial refund, you must use the manual refund method.

Posting Contra Entries

Where you have a customer who is also one of your suppliers, you may offset sales invoices against your supplier's purchase invoices. To do this, you use the Contra Entries option from the Tools menu to match one or more sales invoices with your purchase invoices. Sage 50 will then automatically update the appropriate ledgers. To post a Contra Entry:

Don't forget

If VAT Cash Accounting is being used, make sure the selected transactions have matching tax codes.

1 From the Sage 50 menu click Tools

2 Click on Contra Entries to bring up the Contra Entries window

3 Select Customer (Sales Ledger) and Supplier (Purchase Ledger) accounts

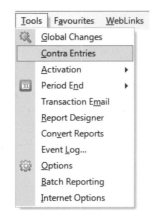

Don't forget

You cannot amend any of the values shown in the Total boxes.

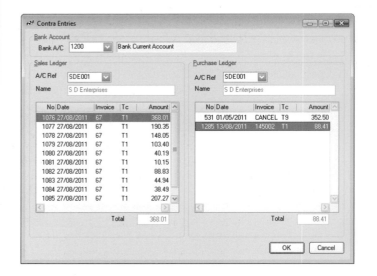

Hot tip

If your totals do not match, a warning message appears asking whether you want to make part-Contra Entries for the lowest amount. If acceptable click the Yes button or No to cancel the Contra Entries.

4 Select outstanding invoice (on sales side) from the list

5 Select invoice to apply Contra Entry for

6 Click OK to finish

Run Period End Functions

Period End options are essential monthly and year end procedures for updating the accounting system. For example, for posting accruals, prepayments and depreciation. The Audit Trail can then be cleared of any unwanted transactions whilst stock can be cleared from your Product history if you so wish.

Through running these procedures, you will also be preparing Sage 50 so that you are ready to enter transactions when you move into a new financial period.

Month End

At each month end it is important to post your prepayments, accruals and depreciation values. Sage 50 will process these transactions automatically and update your nominal account records and Audit Trail for you. The option also exists to clear down your month-to-date turnover figures for your customer and supplier records.

Once you have run the Month End procedures, this is an opportune time to produce some of your financial reports, for example, the Profit and Loss, Balance Sheet, Trial Balance, Budget and Prior Year Analysis reports. Customer statements and Aged analysis reports for Debtors and Creditors will also prove useful.

Month End Guidelines
Here is a check list for the Month End:

- Check all relevant transactions have been posted

- Check recurring entries have been set up and processed

- Check prepayments, accruals and depreciation have been set up

- Complete your bank reconciliation

- Print product history, valuation and profit reports

- Post product journals for your Profit and Loss & Balance Sheet

Hot tip

If program date needs changing for Month End procedure, select Change Program Date from the Settings menu. Remember to re-set the date back to the correct date when done.

Hot tip

Backup your data files before and after running Month End procedures.

169

Hot tip

Use File Maintenance Check and Compress Data options to check your files.

...cont'd

Don't forget

The month end routine is necessary if you have Prepayments, Accruals, Depreciation, or you wish to clear down the turnover figures for Customers and Suppliers.

Hot tip

Always print off your month end reports for future reference.

Hot tip

The Year End is an ideal time to remove any fully paid transactions or unwanted records, leaving only outstanding items on your ledgers at the start of the new Financial Year.

Hot tip

If you have multicompany Sage 50, you can use the Consolidation option from Period End to merge the data from your separate companies to form one set of financial accounts.

After following the Month End guidelines it is time to run the month end procedure. You will probably want to run it on a day other than the actual last calendar day of the month, as this is often more convenient. You will therefore have to change the program date first. To do this, simply follow these steps:

1 First back up your data files

2 From the Sage 50 menu bar click Settings

3 Click on Change Program Date

4 Enter the last day of the month

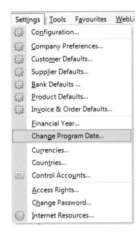

5 Click OK

6 From the Sage 50 menu, click on Tools

7 Select Period End

8 Click on Month End

9 Tick the required options

10 Click OK to run the Month End procedure

Year End

Before you run the Year End, Month End procedures must be completed, together with any final adjustments.

First, when you run Month End on the last month of the current financial year, DO NOT clear the Audit Trail. Once values for the month end have been checked and you are satisfied that they are correct, set the program date to the last date of the current financial year and run Year End:

1 Set the program date to the last day of the financial year by doing Steps 1–5 on Page 170

2 From the Sage 50 menu, click on Tools

3 Select Period End

4 Click on Year End

5 Select here to update your budget figures for each nominal ledger profit and loss account and each product record with the actual values from the year just ending

6 Change Year End Journals Date if necessary

7 Select Output

8 Click OK to run

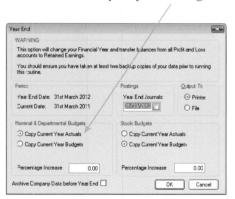

171

Lastly, remove any unwanted Customer, Supplier, Nominal, Bank and Product records and reset system date. You are now ready to continue entering transactions for the new financial year.

Clearing Audit Trail and Stock

This option lets you remove paid and reconciled transactions prior to a specified date from the Audit Trail. This makes the ledgers easier to read. Reconciled transactions on the nominal ledger are brought forward as opening balances.

Sage 50 can store up to 2,000,000,000 transactions in the Audit Trail, so transactions do not have to be removed, but by deleting unwanted transactions, it will free disk space and provide faster access to information.

1 From the Tools menu, select Period End, click Clear Audit Trail, then Next on the first two prompt screens

2 Enter required date

3 Click Next, then Process to clear the Audit Trail

Clear Stock

This option can be run as part of the Month End and Year End procedures. It allows you to decide when to clear transactions from your Product History.

1 From the Tools menu, select Period End, then click Clear Stock

2 Click Yes to continue

3 Enter date here

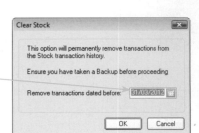

4 Click OK

15 Task Management

This chapter shows you how to use the Diary module for recording meeting or appointment reminders, people to contact, etc. You can quickly view your debtors, record promised payments and even get advice on paying your own bills.

174   Features of the Diary Module

175   The Diary Window

176   Setting Up a Diary Task

177   Setting Up a Recurring Event

178   Completing an Event

179   Chasing Debt

181   Managing Payments

182   Office Integration

185   User Defined Labels

186   Managing Events

Features of the Diary Module

The Diary module makes it easy for you to manage your time and the tasks you need to do. Use the Diary to set up a list of jobs and to prompt you of any that are currently due, overdue or recently completed. By setting up these tasks it acts as a reminder of the actions you need to take to run your business efficiently, helps you liaise with your debtors and saves valuable time.

You can use the Diary to help you:

- Set up a list of tasks that you need to do and also view tasks that are either completed, due or overdue

- List who you need to contact today or in the future, and log any calls you make to customers whilst chasing payment, together with the outcome

- Review bills that are due for payment or overdue

- Check how much you owe your suppliers and, more important, find out how much you are owed by your customers

- Analyse the account status of your customers. For example, you will be able to see at a glance which accounts are overdue, which have been followed up and, when and if payment was promised

- Check your cash flow forecast for a chosen period from information you have set up in Sage 50

- Quickly check for any disputes you may have recorded between yourself and your customers or suppliers, with an easy to read view of the details and reason

- Keep track of payments to suppliers. You can quickly manage all payments due and even tell the Diary how much you can afford to pay at that time, then let the Diary list suggested payments to creditors and if you have enough money in the bank to do so

You can also import appointments from Microsoft®Outlook into the Diary as well as export Diary events and contacts back to Microsoft®Outlook.

Hot tip

To clear an event from the Todo list simply highlight it and click on the Clear button.

Don't forget

To make them easily identifiable, days containing events are highlighted in bold in the calendar.

The Diary Window

The Diary window has a similar layout to the other Sage 50 modules, with Tasks and Links on the left and a toolbar above the Diary view area. The toolbar buttons are used to change the Diary view, as follows:

Day
To Display the Diary in Day View

Work Week
To Display the Diary in Work Week View

Week
To Display the Diary in Week View

Month
To Display the Diary in Month View

Todo List
To Switch to the Todo List View

Diary
To Switch to the Diary View

To bring up the Diary window, do the following:

1 On the Sage 50 menu bar, click Modules

2 Click on Diary

3 Select the view you require

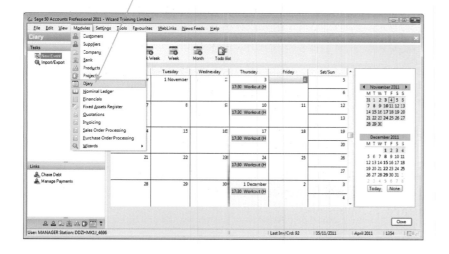

Setting Up a Diary Task

Use the Diary (or Todo option) to create a list of tasks you need to complete. The type of tasks include a general reminder, a meeting or appointment, contact a customer, overdue letters, print management reports, etc. Any additional information that may prove useful can be entered in the Notes box.

Once saved, the task appears on the Diary day and in the Todo list. The Diary/Todo list can then be viewed at any time. To set up a Diary task, proceed as follows:

1 Select the appropriate Diary view

2 Right-click the day required and select Add New Event

3 Enter Subject, Location and Type from the drop down list

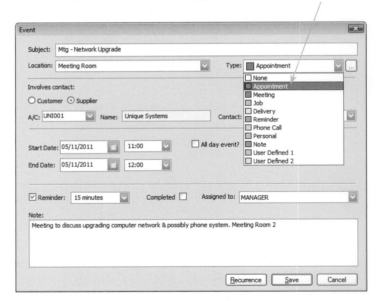

4 Complete the Contact details, Time and Date

5 Set a Reminder so that Sage can inform you when due

6 Type appropriate details in the Note area

7 Click Save for event to appear in the Diary view

Setting Up a Recurring Event

The Diary also allows you to set up a recurring event, such as a regular weekly management meeting, or even a personal event, like an after work session at the Gym, for example.

1 Select the Day view

2 Right-click the time required and select Add New Event

3 Enter Subject, Location and Type from the drop down list

4 Complete the Contact details, Time and Date

5 Set a Reminder and enter details in the Note area

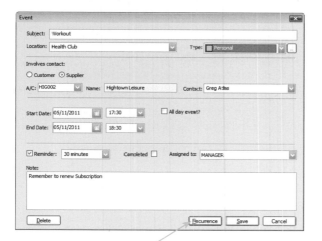

6 Click Recurrence

7 Check details are correct, amend if necessary

8 Click OK, then Save

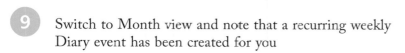

9 Switch to Month view and note that a recurring weekly Diary event has been created for you

Don't forget

When exporting events to Outlook, all instances of a recurring entry will be exported, irrespective of the date range you have chosen.

Hot tip

If you make a mistake when setting up a new event, simply click Delete and start again.

Don't forget

When you have created a recurring entry, always check the Diary and see if any future events fall on days when they cannot take place, e.g. on a bank holiday.

Completing an Event

To Snooze a Reminder

When you have set a Reminder, Sage brings up a window at the appropriate time to prompt you of the approaching event. You can dismiss the reminder or, if there is still more than 15 minutes to go, ask Sage to remind you again nearer the time, as follows:

1 Select the event you wish to be reminded of again later

2 Select how soon you want to be reminded again

3 Click Snooze

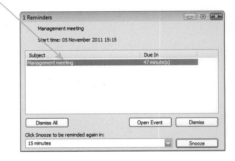

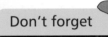
To mark an event as Completed

Once an event has taken place you can either delete it or keep it in the Diary for reference and simply mark it as completed.

1 From the Diary view or Todo List, double-click on the required event to open the event window

2 Click the Completed box

3 Click Save (the Reminder tick is removed automatically)

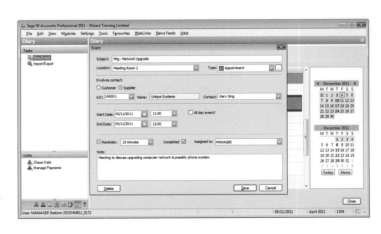

178

Chasing Debt

You can use the Diary to identify who owes you money and record when they promise payment. On the promised date a Sage reminder will then prompt you to check that payment has been received, thus allowing you to keep a close track of your debtors.

To create an automated Promised Payment event

1 From the Links area of the Diary, click Chase Debt to bring up the Chase Debt screen

2 Select a customer with a high Overdue total, then from the Chase Debt toolbar, click Communication

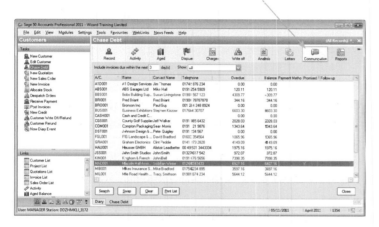

3 When the selected Customer record Communications tab opens click on New

Don't forget

Whenever the Customer record is called up, Sage will remind you if the account is on hold or terms not agreed, etc.

Hot tip

Use the Previous and Next buttons to quickly switch between Customers, if more than one has been selected.

179

Don't forget

Remember to ensure that a search is not applied, otherwise all debtors may not be listed.

...cont'd

4 Contact the customer to discuss how they propose to settle their account. Record the telephone conversation duration with the Telephone Timer, the details of who you spoke to in the Contact Details section, and in the Communication Result section record the details of the payment promised

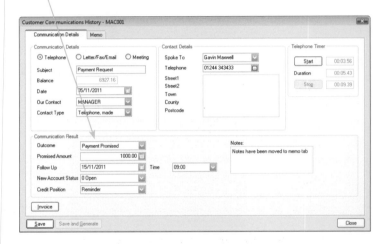

5 Click Save, then Close

6 Close the Customer record and the Chase Debt windows

7 The promised date is now highlighted in the Calendar and an event shown at the top of the Diary for that day

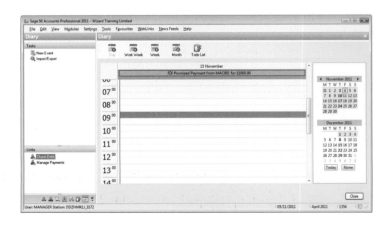

Managing Payments

You can also use the Diary to see which Suppliers you owe money to and to suggest who to pay first and how much, depending on funds available.

1 From the Links area of the Diary, click Manage Payments

2 Click the Suggest Payment button on the toolbar

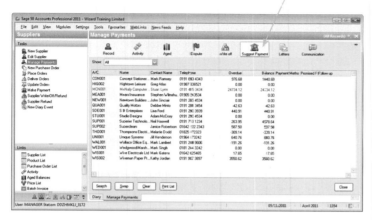

3 A window appears showing what you owe suppliers

4 Enter Funds for Payment here and select a bank account

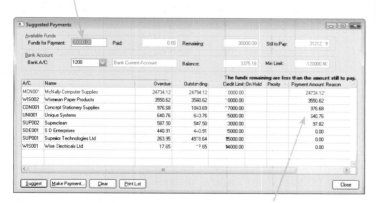

5 Click Suggest to show recommended payments here

6 If you wish to continue and make the suggested payments, click the Make Payment button and go to Page 62

go to Page 62

Hot tip

When working in the Suppliers module, quickly bring up the Manage Payments window by clicking on Manage Payments in the Suppliers Tasks list.

Hot tip

For a printout of all the Suppliers you owe money to, just click the Print List button.

Don't forget

If you leave the Funds for Payment box blank, Sage checks the balance and minimum limit of the bank account you have chosen to see what funds are available and makes a suitable recommendation.

Office Integration

The Sage 50 Diary integrates with Microsoft Outlook. Contacts and events set up in the Diary can be exported to Outlook, whilst appointments can be imported from Outlook into the Diary.

To Import appointments

A handy Wizard helps you easily import events from Outlook:

1 From the File menu, choose Office Integration > Microsoft®Outlook Import/Export Wizard

2 Click OK to bring up the Wizard Welcome window

3 Select Import Outlook Diary Events and click Next

4 Enter a date range for the Outlook events you wish to import and click Next

5 Check your choice of dates in the last screen and then click Finish to start the import

6 Answer any prompts as necessary to complete the import

Note that imported events have a label of None in the Diary. If you wish you can then edit the entry to show a suitable label.

To Export appointments

The Sage 50 Wizard is also used to quickly take you through the steps for exporting your Sage Diary events to Microsoft Outlook, as follows:

1 From the File menu, choose Office Integration > Microsoft®Outlook Import/Export Wizard

2 Click OK to bring up the Wizard Welcome window

3 Select Export Diary Events to Outlook and click Next

4 Enter a date range for the Diary events you wish to export and click Next

5 Check your choice of dates in the last screen and then click Finish to start the export

6 Answer any prompts as necessary to complete the export

Note that as with imported events, exported events have a label of None in Outlook. Again, you can then edit the entry in Outlook to show a suitable label.

...cont'd

To Export Diary Contacts

The third function of the Sage 50 Import / Export Wizard is to quickly help you export your Sage Diary contacts to Microsoft Outlook, as follows:

1 From the File menu, choose Office Integration > Microsoft®Outlook Import/Export Wizard

2 Click OK to bring up the Wizard Welcome window

3 Select Export Contacts to Outlook and click Next

4 Select the Ledgers you wish to export the Diary contacts for and click Next

5 Check your choice in the last screen and then click Finish to start the export

6 Answer any prompts as necessary to complete the export of contacts from Sage to Outlook

If there is a problem during the export, you are returned to Step 4. Click on Change Folder and find the correct Outlook folder.

User Defined Labels

When creating a new Diary event, Sage provides you with a handy drop-down list of pre-defined event types to choose from.

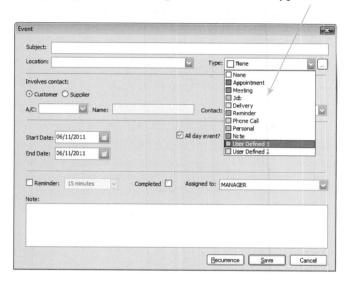

Hot tip

To show an event as lasting all day, just click the All day event box.

However, the last two in the list are reserved for the user to define as follows:

1 Select the appropriate Diary view

2 Right-click the day required and select Add New Event

3 Enter a Subject and Location

4 Click here, to the right of the Type box

Don't forget

When you place a tick in the All day event box, the start and end time entry boxes become hidden, and vice versa.

5 Type a name for either the first, or both, labels

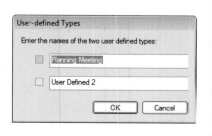

6 Click OK, then choose your new label and click Save

Managing Events

To View events

Use the Todo list view to quickly see Diary events already set up.

1 From the Diary toolbar, click the Todo button

2 Choose the required Diary view, e.g. Month

3 All events for that period are displayed

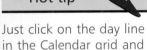

Hot tip

Just click on the day line in the Calendar grid and start typing to add a quick diary note.

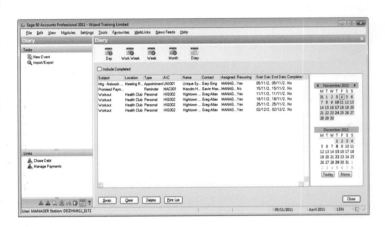

To Delete an event

You would normally leave events in the Diary for reference. To delete an event, however, such as a cancelled meeting:

1 From the Diary toolbar, click the Todo button and choose the required view

2 Select the event or task you want to delete

3 Click Delete

Hot tip

To quickly reschedule an appointment or meeting simply drag it to the new day and time line. The details are amended automatically for you.

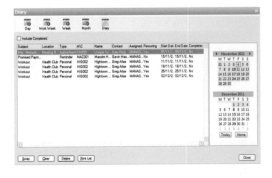

Index

A

Account Status	14
Accruals	53
Activity	
Customer	23
Supplier	37
Adjustments In	84
Adjustments Out	84
Aged Balances	38
Customer	23
Supplier	38
All Day Event	185
Allocating Stock	105
Assemblies	80
Asset	
Depreciation	137
Valuation	138
Audit Trail	121–122
Clearing the Audit Trail	172
Automated Promised Payment	179

B

Backing Up	156
Balance Sheet	125
Bank	57–72
Account Types	59
Bank, Cash and Credit	60
Batch Purchase Payments	63
Cheques	68
Customer Receipts	65
Payments	61
Print Bank Remittances Button	58, 62
Receipts	64
Reconciliation	70–71
Making Adjustments	71
Recurring Entries	67
Reports	72
Statement	69
Supplier Invoice Payments	62
Toolbar	58
Transfers	66
Bank Account	
Opening Balances	152–153
Reconciliation	70–71
Bank Statement	69
Bank Transfers	66
Bar Code	77

B (continued)

Batch	
Customer Credit Notes	26
Customer Invoices	25
Supplier Credit Notes	40
Supplier Invoices	39
Bill of Materials	80
Budget Report	127

C

Calculations	139
Calendar	174–175, 180, 186
Camera Button	47
Cash Account	60
Cash Flow	72
Categories	
Fixed Assets	12, 135
Products	12, 75
Changing Program Date	170
Chart of Accounts	54–55
Chasing Debt	179
Check Button	55
Cheque Returns	167
Cheques	68
Clearing Opening Balances	149
Clearing Stock	172
Comma Separated Values	160
Communication Button	179
Communication Result	180
Company Preferences	12
Completing an Event	178
Configuration Editor	12–14, 18
Consolidation	170
Contacts	22, 184
Contra Entries	168
Control Accounts	17
Copy Matrix Button	81
Correcting Transactions	163
Corruption of Data	156
Credit	50
Credit Card Account	60
Credit Charges	28
Credit Control	22, 35
Credit Note	40
Product	96
Service	97
Criteria	139
CSV (Comma Separated Values) Files	160
Currency	15
Current Liquidity	126

Customer Activity   23
Customer Defaults   16
Customer Ledger   19–32
    Activity   23
    Batch Credit Notes   26
    Batch Invoices   25
    Debtors Analysis   27
    Disputed Invoices   29
    Labels   31
    Letters   31
    Phone   30
    Price List   24
    Records   22–23
    Reports   30
    Statement   32
    Toolbar   21

D

Dashboard   10
Data Compression   164
Data Management   155–172
    Backing Up   156
    Clearing Stock   172
    Clearing the Audit Trail   172
    File Maintenance   162–164
    Global Values   158–159
    Importing Data   160–161
    Period End Functions   169–171
    Restoring Data   157
    Write Off, Refund and Return 165–167
Data Protection Act   11
Day Books   72
Debit   50
Debtors Analysis   27
Defaults
    Customer   16
    Product   17
    Supplier   16
Delete Events   186
Delivery Addresses   12
Depreciation   137
    Reducing Balance   135
    Straight Line   135
    Write Off   135
Desktop Views   10
    Dashboard   10
    List Display   10
    Process Map   10
Despatching Sales Orders   106
Diary   173–186

Add New Event   176
Automated Promised Payment   179
Chasing Debt   179
Completing an Event   178
Contacts   184
Delete an Event   186
Export Appointments   183
Import Appointments   182
Managing Events   186
Managing Payments   181
Note   186
Notes Box   176
Office Integration   182
Recurring Event   177
Reminder   176
Reschedule   186
Snooze a Reminder   178
Task   176
Todo Option   176
User Defined Labels   185
View Events   186
Views   175
Diary Note   186
Discard Button   61
Disputed Invoices   29
Double-Entry Bookkeeping   50

E

E-Banking   131
E-Submissions Credentials   131
E-VAT Submissions   131
Easy Startup Wizard   12
Email   88, 103, 115
Error Checking   162
Error Corrections   163
Euro   15
Event Types   185
Excel   72
Exchange Rates   15
Export   183

F

F11 Key   30
File Maintenance   162
Filters   139
Finance Rates   18
Financials   119–132

Audit Trail	121–122
Balance Sheet	125
Budget Report	127
Printing the Audit Trail	122
Profit and Loss Report	124
Quick Ratio	126
Recording your Fixed Assets	135
Reports	132
Toolbar	120
Trial Balance	123
VAT Return	128–130
VAT Transfer Wizard	130
Financial Systems	20
Financial Year	14
Finder Button	30
Fixed Assets	133–138
Depreciation	137
Fixed Asset Records	136
Toolbar	134
Valuation	138
Fixed Assets Categories	12
Footer Details	91
Frequency Details	97
Funds for Payment	181

G

GDN (Goods Delivery Note)	102, 106
Getting Started	7–18
Company Preferences	12
Currency & the Euro	15
Customer & Supplier Defaults	16
Finance Rates	18
Introduction	8
Settings	11
Starting Sage Line 50	9
Global Changes	81
Global Values	158
Government Gateway Account	128, 131
Graphs	47
GRN (Goods Received Note)	110, 114–116
Grouping	141

H

HM Revenue and Customs	20, 128, 165

I

Import	182
Import / Export Wizard	182–184
Importing Data	160
Internet Access	128
Intrastat (Arrivals Confirmation)	110, 117
Intrastat (Despatches Confirmation)	102, 104
Introduction	8
Invoices	87–100
Printing an Invoice	92
Printing Batch Invoices	99
Product	90–91
Product Credit Note	96
Reports	100
Service	93–94
Service Credit Note	97
Skeleton	95
Toolbar	88
Updating	98

J

Journal	50
Credit	50
Debit	50
Journal Entry	51
Skeleton Journals	50

L

Labels	31, 41
Layout and Format	139
Letters	31, 41
List Display	10

M

Make Payment Button	181
Making Adjustments	71
Managing Events	186
Managing Payments	181
Memorised Invoices	97
Message	90

Microsoft Outlook	182–184
Modifying an Existing Report	144
Month End	169–170
Guidelines	169
Procedure	170
Multicompany Consolidation	170
Multiple Document Windows	140

N

Navigation Bar	22, 35, 45, 59
New	
Customer Wizard	22
Nominal Account Wizard	45
Report	141
Supplier Wizard	35
Nominal Ledger	43–56
Accruals	53
Activity	48
Chart of Accounts	54–55
Graphs	47
Making a Journal Entry	51
Nominal Accounts	45
Opening Balances	152
Prepayments	52
Records	46
Reports	56
Reversals	50
The Journal	50
Toolbar	44
Transaction Codes/Types	49
Viewing Nominal Transactions	47–49
Nominal Ledger Reversals Button	44

O

Office Integration	182
Online Filing	20
Online VAT Payment	131
Online VAT Submission	131
On Order	113
Opening Balances	145–154
Brought Forward	172
Clearing O/B From Trial Balance	149–150
Entering O/B during the Year	151
Introduction	146
Nominal Ledger and Bank Account	152–153
Products	154

Standard VAT	147
VAT Cash Accounting	148
Order Details	91
Outlook	177, 182–184

P

Page Footer	142
Page Header	142
Part Payment	63
Passwords	11
Payments	57
Batch Purchase	63
Supplier Invoice	62
To Bank	61
Period End Functions	169
Petty Cash	60
Phone	30
Placing Orders Manually	115
Prepayments	52
Pre-Printed Stationery	140
Previewing your Report	143
Price Lists	16, 24
Print Bank Remittances Button	58
Printing	
Batched Purchase Orders	117
Invoice	92
Invoices	
Batch Invoices	99
Sales Orders	107
Process Map	10
Products	73–86
Activity	82
Adjustments	84
Bill of Materials (BOM)	80
Categories	12
Defaults	17, 78
Discounts	81
Opening Balances	154
Record	75–77
Reports	86
Shortfall Generator Button	74, 85
Toolbar	74
Transfers	85
Using Search	79
Viewing Transactions	81
Profit and Loss Report	124
Promised Payment	179
Purchase Order Deliveries	
Recording Deliveries	114
Purchase Order Processing	109–118
Goods Received Note Button	110

Manual Deliveries	116
On Order	113
Place Manually On Order	115
Printing	117
Purchase Order	111–112
Reports	118
Toolbar	110

Q

Quick Ratio	126

R

Rebuild	164
Recall Button	95
Receipts	
Bank	64
Customer	65
Recording Deliveries Manually	116
Recording Stock Deliveries Automatically	114
Records	
Bank	59
Customer	22
Nominal	46
Product	75
Supplier	35
Recurring Button	95
Recurring Entries	67
Recurring Event	177
Refunds	165
ReIndex	164
Reminder	176
Remittance Button	62
Report Designer	139–144
Calculations	139
Creating a new Report	141
Criteria	139
Filters	139
Grouping	141
Introduction	140
Layout and Format	139
Modifying an existing Report	144
Printing	140
Report Wizard	141
Sort Variables	141
Stationery	140
Totals	142

Reports	
Bank	72
Customer	30
Financial	132
Fixed Assets	135
Invoicing	100
Nominal	56
Products	86
Purchase Orders	118
Sales Orders	108
Suppliers	42
Report Variables	141
Reschedule	186
Restoring Data	157
Returns	165, 167
Reversals	50

S

Sage 50 Desktop	9
Sales Order Processing	101–108
Allocating Stock	105
Amending	107
Despatching	106
Printing	107
Reports	108
Sales Order	103–104
Toolbar	102
Search	36, 49, 79
Service Credit Note	97
Service Invoice	93–94
Settings	11
Account Status	14
Company Preferences	12
Control Accounts	17
Currency	15
Customer Defaults	16
Finance Rates	18
Financial Year	14
Fixed Assets	12
Passwords	11
Product Defaults	17
Products	12
Supplier Defaults	16
Tax Codes	13
Shortcut Keys	11
Shortfall Generator	74, 85
Skeleton Invoice	95
Skeleton Journals	50
Snooze a Reminder	178
Special Product Item	90
Standard VAT Opening Balances	147

Start up check List	8
Statement	32
Stationery	140
Stock	
Allocation	105
Clearing Stock	172
Stock Take Details	76
Stock Take Option	75
Suggest Button	181
Suggest Payment	181
Supplier Defaults	16
Supplier Ledger	33–42
Activity	37
Aged Balance	38
Batch Invoices	39
Credit Note	40
Labels	41
Letters	41
Records	35
Reports	42
Toolbar	34
Using Search	36

T

Task Management	173–186
Automated Promised Payment	179
Chasing Debt	179
Completing an Event	178
Delete an Event	186
Diary Module	174
Diary Task	176
Diary Views	175
Diary Window	175
Export Appointments	183
Features of the Diary Module	174
Import Appointments	182
Managing Events	186
Managing Payments	181
Office Integration	182
Recurring Event	177
Snooze a Reminder	178
Todo List	186
Todo Option	176
View Events	186
Tax Codes	13
Telephone Timer	180
Telephoning your Customer	30
Today Button	175
Todo Button	186
Todo List	186

Transaction Types	23, 37, 49, 82
Customer	23
Nominal	49
Product	82
Supplier	37
Trial Balance	123
Clearing Opening Balances	149

U

Updating your Ledgers	98
User Defined Labels	185

V

Valuation of Fixed Assets	138
VAT Cash Accounting Opening Balances	148
VAT Numbers	12, 22
VAT Return	128–130
VAT Transfer Wizard	130
Verify Button	129
View Events	186
Viewing Transactions	37, 47, 81
Views	10

W

Windows Desktop	9
Wizards	
Bank Account	58
Customer	22
Easy Startup Wizard	12
Nominal Account	45
Supplier	35
VAT Transfer Wizard	130
Write Off, Refund and Return	165–167
Write Offs	167
www.hmrc.gov.uk	20
WWW Details	12, 22, 35

Y

Year End Procedure	171